Language and the Teacher:
A Series in Applied Linguistics

Volume 4

under the editorial direction of

DR. ROBERT C. LUGTON

American Language Institute of New York University

LANGUAGE AND THE TEACHER:
A SERIES IN APPLIED LINGUISTICS

The series will be concerned with the following areas—

GENERAL STUDIES
Psycholinguistics, sociolinguistics, bilingualism.

GRAMMAR
Morphology, syntax, contrastive structure.

PHONOLOGY
Phonemics, intonation, contrastive phonetics, etc.

VOCABULARY STUDIES
Frequency counts, production and principles, lexicology.

READING SKILLS
Beginning skills, development, construction of texts,
literary reading.

WRITING SKILLS
Beginning skills, development, composition.

METHODOLOGY
Evaluation of methods, techniques, classroom practices.

LANGUAGE TEACHING
FOR DIFFERENT AGE GROUPS
Elementary, secondary, college, adult.

MACHINE TEACHING
Programmed learning, audio-visual equipment and
software, language laboratory.

TEACHER EDUCATION
Standards and evaluation, projects, curricula for
teacher training

ADMINISTRATION
Curriculum development, articulation, public relations.

TESTING
Techniques, statistical studies.

BIOGRAPHY

BIBLIOGRAPHY

ENGLISH AS A SECOND LANGUAGE

METHODS OF RESEARCH IN LINGUISTICS
AND LANGUAGE TEACHING

Language and the Teacher:
A Series in Applied Linguistics

Improving Achievement in Foreign Language

by Robert L. Politzer
and
Louis Weiss

both of the School of Education,
Stanford University

THE CENTER FOR CURRICULUM DEVELOPMENT, INC.
401 Walnut Street   Philadelphia, Pa.

#2578

Originally issued as Final Report: An Experiment in Improving Achievement in Foreign Language through Learning of Selected Skills Associated with Language Aptitude. Stanford Center for Research and Development in Teaching pursuant to a contract with the Office of Education, H.E.W. (Contract No. OEC 4-6-051097-1231)

Acknowledgments

The investigators would like to express their gratitude to all those who made possible the experiments which are reported herewith. Thanks are due to the teachers and high-school students whose classes were used in Phase I of the experiment and to the staff and officials of the Defense Language Institute (West Coast Branch) for allowing experiments to be conducted in conjunction with their training program. We also wish to acknowledge the help given by Dr. Michio P. Hagiwara and Mrs. Karen Kvavik in the construction of the training materials used in Phase I and by Dr. Carl Rinne, Mr. John Duncan, and Mr. Philip Sedlak in the administration of the experiment and the evaluation of the results of that phase of the study.

Phase II of the study was conducted in the Palo Alto Unified School District, and the investigators wish to express their particular thanks to the teachers of the Palo Alto schools who cooperated in the writing of the training materials and whose classes took part in the experiment. Particular thanks are due to the administration of the Palo Alto Unified School District and especially to the Director of Research, Dr. Bruce Keepes. The investigators are also indebted to Dr. Janet Elashoff of the Methodology Unit of the Stanford Center for Research and Development in Teaching for advice and assistance with the statistical treatment of the experimental data.

ROBERT L. POLITZER
Principal Investigator

LOUIS WEISS
Assistant Investigator

Table of Contents

List of Tables

List of Figures

Figure Page

Abstract

The purpose of the experiment was two-fold. It was designed to determine whether foreign-language aptitude as measured by standard foreign-language aptitude tests (Pimsleur LAB, Carroll-Sapon MLAT) could be significantly increased by specific training and whether increases in language aptitude brought about by such training resulted in better achievement in foreign-language study.

The experiment was conducted in two phases. For the first phase of the experiment, training materials based primarily on the MLAT and dealing essentially with sound-symbol relation and awareness of structure in English were prepared. The training materials were used in the Defense Language Institute West (Monterey) as well as in various high schools in the San Francisco Bay area. Selected language classes were used as experimental training groups, and their achievement on post-tests in language aptitude and on criterion tests in the foreign language was compared with the achievement of control groups which were not exposed to the aptitude training. The post-tests did not show clear-cut differences between experimental and control groups on either language achievement or aptitude tests. They did indicate, however, that both experimental and control groups showed gains in language aptitude which were significantly larger than those which might be due to any retest effect.

The training materials used for the second phase of the experiment were based primarily on the Pimsleur Language Aptitude Battery and emphasized the development of inductive language learning and reasoning ability. The second phase of the experiment was conducted in the Palo Alto Unified School District with three pairs of first-year Junior High School classes (2 Spanish, 2 German and 2 French). The experimental classes received aptitude training while the control classes were exposed to cultural materials. Both the aptitude training and the cultural material training took place concurrently with initial training in the foreign language. In addition, the aptitude training was also offered to a group of classes which concentrated on the acquisition of study skills rather than on the study of any specific foreign language.

The experiment showed that all classes involved (Experimental, Control and Study Skills) made gains in language aptitude which could not be accounted for by a simple retest effect. In addition, there was a general tendency for experimental classes to achieve somewhat higher than control classes on both the second aptitude test and the language achievement tests which were administered as part of the experiment. This tendency was particularly pronounced among male subjects. The difference in achievement of male experimental subjects over male control subjects on the LAB post-test almost reached the .05 level of significance and on at least one of the language tests (Final Achievement in Spanish) male experimental subjects performed significantly better than male control subjects ($p < .05$). The experiment indicates that specific training in language aptitude may very well be an important educational tool, though it is probably most effective if undertaken before any exposure to foreign-language learning.

Introduction

FOREIGN LANGUAGE APTITUDE AND APTITUDE TRAINING

The nature of foreign-language aptitude has been under rather intensive investigation during the past fifteen years. Most of the work concerning the measurement of aptitude has been done by two researchers, John B. Carroll and Paul Pimsleur, working either independently or in collaboration with others. Both have summarized their work concerning foreign-language aptitude in recent publications (Carroll, 1962, 1965; Pimsleur, 1966) which also contain fairly complete bibliographies concerning research on language aptitude. Both researchers, Paul Pimsleur and John B. Carroll (the latter in association with Stanley Sapon), have developed test batteries for the purpose of predicting success in foreign-language study. The Pimsleur Language Aptitude Battery (LAB) consists of the following subtests (Pimsleur, 1966, pp. 179-180):

1. Grade point average of the student.

2. A five-point scale on which the student indicates his interest in foreign-language study.

3. Vocabulary: This includes 24 items of vocabulary. The student is required to select from a group of four synonyms the word that most nearly means the same as the stimulus word.

4. Language Analysis: This includes 15 items. The student is given vocabulary and some model sentences in a foreign language together with fifteen sentences in English. The student is required to select from among four choices the foreign-language sentence which is the correct translation of the stimulus sentence.

5. Sound Discrimination: This includes 30 items. The student is taught three words in Ewe, a language of Nigeria, which differ minimally in pitch, nasality, and non-nasality. He is required to indicate on his answer sheet which of the three words is heard in a short sentence presented on audio-tape.

6. Sound-Symbol Association: This includes 24 items of nonsense words spoken on audio-tape. The student is required to select from four words very similar in spelling the correct symbolic representation of the stimulus word.

The Carroll-Sapon Modern Language Aptitude Test (MLAT, Carroll-Sapon, 1958) consists of the following sub-tests:

1. Number Learning: This includes 15 items with a value of three points each. The student is taught by tape the number system of an artificial language. He is then required to write down in arabic numerals the numbers which he hears presented on tape.

2. Phonetic Script: This includes 30 items. The student learns the phonetic symbols corresponding to some English phonemes by listening to words and following their transcriptions in the test booklet. He is then required to identify the correct phonemic transcription of the English words from a choice of two similar transcriptions presented in the test booklet.

3. Spelling Clues: This includes 50 items. A word is spelled in an unusual and/or abbreviated form. The student indicates that he has been able to recognize the word by identifying a synonym or near-synonym from among five choices.

4. Words in Sentences: This includes 45 items. Each item consists of two or three sentences in English. In the first sentence, one word is printed in capital letters. In the following sentences, several words are underlined and identified by numbers. The student must choose the word that has the same

grammatical function as the word printed in capital letters in the first sentence.

5. Paired Associates: This includes 24 items. The student is asked to study a list of 24 English-Foreign-Language equivalents and is then examined on his retention of vocabulary by a multiple-choice test.

Carroll (Carroll, 1958, 1962) has tried to identify the specific factors involved in foreign-language aptitude and has come to the conclusion that they can be considered under four headings: (1) phonetic coding; (2) grammatical sensitivity; (3) rote memory; (4) inductive learning ability.

(1) Phonetic coding is defined by Carroll as the "ability to 'code' auditory phonetic material in such a way that this material can be recognized, identified, and remembered over something longer than a few seconds." (Carroll, 1962, p. 128). This phonetic coding ability is evidently tested in parts 1 and 2 of the Carroll-Sapon MLAT (and possibly in part 3 of the MLAT) and in parts 5 and 6 of the Pimsleur LAB. In addition, part 3 of the MLAT and part 6 of the LAB also test an ability that one might call flexibility in perceiving sound-symbol relationships.

(2) Grammatical sensitivity is definitely tested in part 4 of the MLAT and may also be involved in part 4 of the LAB.

(3) Rote memory is the aspect of foreign-language learning examined in part 5 (and probably part 1) of the MLAT, but does not seem to be represented in the Pimsleur tests.

(4) Inductive learning ability is measured quite obviously in part 4 of the Pimsleur LAB, but is not represented in the MLAT although it was found in earlier versions of aptitude tests developed by Carroll and Sapon (and, among others, in the Army Language Aptitude Test. See Carroll, 1962).

We can see, therefore, that there is a certain amount of agreement in the way in which the two test batteries define and approach language aptitude. There are also some differences: the Pimsleur test battery includes such items as grade point average and interest in foreign-language study which measure the student's general willingness to learn—but do not tell us very much about the specific aptitudes. Unlike the present MLAT, the Pimsleur LAB approaches the inductive learning ability quite directly (in part 4) and includes a test on sound discrimination which is less directly approached by the MLAT but may indeed be involved in part 1 of the MLAT. The Pimsleur battery does not include any measure of rote memory, although it is quite possible that parts 5 and 6 may correspond to the aspect of language learning which requires rote memory. We can compare the process of speaking a foreign language to a sort of "manufacturing process" in which the student converts utterances which he has committed to memory into new material: i.e., sentences and utterances of his own (Politzer, 1965, p. 137). The manufacturing process is the part of foreign-language learning which requires the grammatical sensitivity and the inductive learning abilities. But the prerequisite of the manufacturing process is the availability of raw materials—of utterances which the student has retained in his memory. This prerequisite depends on the student's memory (MLAT, part 5) or his willingness and eagerness to learn (LAB, parts 1 and 2).

The question of the relative validity of the Pimsleur LAB and the MLAT (considered by Pimsleur, 1966, p. 179) is not of paramount importance in this context, especially since they seem to agree as far as the major components of language aptitude are concerned. The main problem with which this research project is concerned is not the prediction of success but whether some of the components of language aptitude (as identified by the MLAT and LAB) are subject to modification by training, and whether this training can, in turn, result in higher achievement. The view that aptitudes do not necessarily represent consistent biologically determined characteristics but are, to a large extent, subject to modification by learning is held by many psychologists. (For a classical statement of this opinion, see Ferguson, 1954, 1956.) The concept that aptitudes can be modified by training is, to some extent at least, implied in the transfer of learning argument. If we, for instance, hold that students who have studied a foreign language will learn another foreign language more easily than an equal group not exposed to prior foreign-language training, we are in fact stating that language training results in an improvement in foreign-language aptitude.

Attempts to show increase in aptitude and performance as a result of prior foreign-language study have so far, at least, not been entirely successful (Carroll, 1963, p. 109; Sturgis, 1966). As far as attempts to increase measurable language aptitude through specific training are concerned, we are aware of only two such undertakings (Yeni-Komshian, 1965; Hatfield, 1965).

Grace Yeni-Komshian attempted in her doctoral dissertation (Yeni-Komshian, 1965) to give specific training in auditory perception skills in order to improve the related language aptitude measures of an experimental group of students. In her study, she compared an experimental group which received training in auditory discrimination with a control group which received no training. Pre- and post-test measures included among others, parts 2 and 3 of the MLAT. The study furnished some indication that scores on aptitude measures could be improved by training, but did not answer the important question whether improvement of measurable aptitudes brought about by such training also had some effect on achievement in foreign language.

William N. Hatfield, in his doctoral dissertation (Hatfield, 1965), identified a group of students considered to be underachievers in the auditory skills (as measured by the Pimsleur LAB) and presented a series of half-hour lessons designed to improve these skills to an experimental group of students. The language grades of the experimental group were compared to those of a matched control group at the end of the first semester, and it was found that the grades of the experimental group were significantly higher than those of the control group. Unfortunately, it was found that this significant difference did not persist throughout the school year, so that the results of this study are somewhat ambiguous.

The research reported herewith thus addresses itself to the following problems:

1. Is it possible to increase language aptitude through specific training?
2. Does an increase in aptitude brought about through specific training truly reflect a higher learning ability as measured by success in foreign-language study?

3. Does foreign-language training as such increase measurable language aptitude?

The Language-Aptitude experiment was conducted in two distinct phases over a period of three years. In the first phase (which was conducted in 1966-67) the Carroll-Sapon MLAT and the Army Language-Aptitude Test were used as measures of increase in aptitude, while in the second phase (conducted in 1968-69) the Pimsleur LAB was used. Achievement in foreign language study was measured by criterion tests constructed especially for the experiment. These tests and the specially designed training materials will be made available by the principal investigator upon request.

Phase I of the Experiment

Experimental Design

Since this was essentially an exploratory, pilot study, the design was a rather simple Experimental-Control Group model consisting of comparable pairs of classes with each pair studying the same language with the same teacher. The Experimental Groups received the aptitude training either before or during the initial phase of their foreign-language study, while the Control Group received no aptitude training at all. Thus, the aptitude training was the only independent variable of the experiment. The dependent variables were the measures of language aptitude and the measures of achievement in the foreign language.

This phase of the experiment was carried out in two very different teaching situations, namely: three high schools located in the San Francisco Bay area and the West Coast Branch of the Defense Language Institute.

Training Program

The training program that was devised in conjunction with this phase of the experiment was based on the characteristics of aptitude as revealed by the Carroll-Sapon aptitude tests.

The components of aptitude considered in the program were: Auditory Discrimination, Sound-Symbol Relation. Phonetic Coding, Grammatical Sensitivity, and Inductive Learning Ability. A description of the training materials and tests devised for each of these components follows.

Auditory Discrimination.—Three training tapes were recorded. Each tape provided discrimination training of the "Same vs. Different" type. The sound differences utilized were either non-phonemic in English or were presented in positions in which they were non-phonemic in English. The sound contrasts used in the training procedures were the following:

Tape #1: 1) š/ž (Voiced/unvoiced alveopalatal fricatives)
2) ts/č (Alveolar/alveopalatal affricated stops)
3) n/ŋ (Dental/velar nasal)
4) q/k (Voiced/unvoiced uvular stops)

Tape #2: 1) e/ey (Monophthong/diphthong)
2) o/ow (Monophthong/diphthong)
3) a/ã (Oral vowel/nasal vowel)
4) u/w (Rounded/unrounded back vowels)

Tape #3: 1) Rising tone/level tone
2) Falling-rising tone/falling tone
3) High-level tone/rising tone
4) Falling tone/falling-rising tone

Each exercise consisted of 25 items arranged in five groups, each group containing five items. Difficulty was increased from group to group by increasing the syllable length of the sound sequence to be differentiated as well as the number of items from among which the discrimination had to be made. Each tape was followed by a short test of 8 items dealing with the sound discriminations taught on the tape.

Elements of Language Structure.—In addition to the Auditory Discrimination tapes, a booklet entitled "Elements of Language Structure" was developed. The booklet was written in the form of a program, so that it could be used for self-instruction. Answers to each frame were provided in the following frame. The booklet contained three parts: (1) The Sounds of

English; (2) The Structure of English; (3) Learning Language Structure. These parts of the booklet correspond to aspects of language aptitude as follows:

Sound-Symbol Relationship.— In part 1 of the booklet there are 168 steps or frames in which the main principles of articulatory phonetics and phonemic transcriptions are explained. Phonemic symbols for the segmental phonemes of English are introduced. At the same time, the student learns how the same phonemes can have different orthographic representation. The 168 frames explaining sound-symbol relations are followed by 182 frames in which the student practices phonemic transcriptions of English words.

Sound-Symbol Relationship and Phonetic Coding.—After the practice in transcribing words from regular orthography, the student receives training in using phonemic transcription from taped dictation of 100 items of which there are 70 English words and 30 "English" nonsense syllables.

Grammatical Sensitivity.— Part 2 of the training booklet consists of 222 steps of frames dealing with the "Structure of English." The student is taught the major concepts of structural relationships (word order; function words vs. lexical words; significance of morphological endings; concept of "pattern" substitution classes of English; etc.).

Inductive Learning Ability.—Part 3 of the training booklet contains 50 frames showing, by some simple examples taken from Japanese, how the meaning of forms and structural arrangements can be inferred from other forms.

In connection with the training booklets, two tests—one for Sounds of English (20 items) and one for the Structure of English (25 items)—were developed. The tests are of the multiple-choice type and are based strictly on the material taught in parts 1 and 2 of the training program. Since the experiment took place under actual field conditions, it was not always possible to administer all the tests that would have been of interest. As we shall point out later, it was also not possible to receive complete sets of all experimental data from all the classes taking part in the high-school experiment. The following data were gathered from the Experimental and Control Groups.

Defense Language Institute Experiment

Five classes—trainees in Spanish, Russian, Vietnamese, Chinese, and Arabic—took part in the experiment. All classes were divided into Experimental and Control Groups which were evenly matched by initial aptitude scores. For each of the groups, the following data were obtained:

Experimental Group	*Control Group*
Army Language Aptitude Test (Pre-test)	Army Language Aptitude Test (Pre-test)
Training Program Auditory Discrimination Test #1 Test #2 Test #3 Sounds of English Test Structure of English Test	No Training Program Given
Foreign-Language Progress Test #1 Test #2 Test #3 Test #4	Foreign-Language Progress Test #1 Test #2 Test #3 Test #4
Six-weeks Grades	Six-weeks Grades
Army Language Aptitude Test (Post-test)	Army Language Aptitude Test (Post-test)

High-School Experiment

Seven pairs of first-year foreign-language classes (3 French, 3 Spanish, 1 German) were used in this experiment. Each pair was taught by the same teacher, and all classes taking part in the experiment used the *A-LM* text *(Audio-Lingual Materials:* Harcourt, Brace and World, Inc.) for their first year of foreign-language instruction. Although it was impossible to assign students to classes at random, the classes themselves were randomly assigned to either Experimental or Control treatment.

An approximately even balance between boys and girls existed in both the Experimental and the Control Groups. For each of the groups, the following data were obtained:

Experimental Group	*Control Group*
Modern Language—	Modern Language—
Aptitude Test	Aptitude Test
(Carroll-Sapon)	(Carroll-Sapon)
(Pre-test, parts 1-5)	(Pre-test, parts 1-5)
Training Program	No Training Program Given
Auditory Discrimination	
Test #1	
Test #2	
Test #3	
Sounds of English Test	
Structure of English Test	
Foreign-Language Progress	Foreign-Language Progress
Test #1	Test #1
Test #2	Test #2
Test #3	Test #3
Modern Language—	Modern Language—
Aptitude Test	Aptitude Test
(Carroll-Sapon)	(Carroll-Sapon)
(Post-test, parts 2, 3,	(Post-test, parts 2, 3,
4 only)	4 only)

Although the complete set of data could be obtained from only four of the seven pairs of classes, all data gathered will be considered in the discussion.

Progress Tests

The Progress Tests were designed and written especially for the experiment. Each of the Progress Tests consisted of three multiple-choice sub-tests:

Part A: 15 items. This is a test of understanding of the sound-symbol relation in the foreign language being studied.

Part B: 15 items. This is a test of understanding of the structure of the foreign language being studied.

Part C: 20 items. This test is very similar to Part B and was designed to measure the student's understanding and grasp of the grammar in the units covered in classroom instruction.

The three batteries of Progress Tests were designed to be administered after units 5, 7, and 9 of the *A-LM* materials and were given in January, March and May of the school year.

Post-tests

It should be noted that only parts 2, 3, and 4 of the MLAT were administered as post-tests. The decision to omit parts 1 and 5 was due to the lack of available time at the end of the school year. It was felt that scores on those parts of the test would also be least likely to be affected by the training procedures. No special final exam was designed for the classes taking part in the experiment, since the third progress test was taken very near the time of the final examination. Also, the administration of a specially designed final-criterion measure would have run into technical difficulties (lack of time at the end of the school year).

RESULTS AND DISCUSSION

DEFENSE LANGUAGE INSTITUTE EXPERIMENT

Table 1 summarizes the mean scores obtained in the Defense Language Institute Experiment. As can be seen from this table, the only significant difference between Experimental and Control Groups on these criteria occurred in the Vietnamese groups, where the Control Group performed better than the Experimental Group on the six-weeks examination. Due to the differences in length of the language programs themselves, the Spanish classes were the only ones presenting data on the final examinations at the conclusion of this phase of the study. In these classes, the Experimental Groups performed slightly better than the Control Group with a mean score of 86.58 as compared to a mean score of 83.27. A t-test of significance of differences between means yielded a $p < .10$. These results gave some indication that the skills learned in the experimental training may be of some use in learning a language

TABLE 1

Defense Language Institute Experiment: Summary of Mean Scores for All Classes

	Spanish		Chinese		Arabic		Russian		Vietnamese		All Languages Combined	
	Exper. (N=18)	Control (N=19)	Exper. (N=20)	Control (N=27)	Exper. (N=10)	Control (N=9)	Exper. (N=54)	Control (N=57)	Exper. (N=16)	Control (N=17)	Exper. (N=118)	Control (N=129)
Army Aptitude (Pre-test)	30.50	31.26	38.90	36.12	41.50	41.77	34.24	33.25	32.13	33.00	34.78	34.09
Auditory Discrim. 1	7.50	—	7.20	—	7.50	—	7.33	—	7.31	—	7.34	—
Auditory Discrim. 2	6.38	—	6.75	—	6.50	—	6.37	—	6.56	—	6.47	—
Auditory Discrim. 3	7.11	—	7.10	—	7.60	—	6.66	—	5.12	—	6.94	—
Sounds of English	16.88	—	17.18	—	18.25	—	18.27	—	17.06	—	17.81	—
Structure of English	19.22	—	19.95	—	20.78	—	20.85	—	19.56	—	20.26	—
Six-weeks Grades	88.29	89.00	82.82	83.29	87.70	89.33	79.27	80.06	86.67	89.73	83.28	84.35
Army Aptitude (Post-test)	43.47	42.06	45.86	41.31	43.00	48.33	39.95	42.05	39.93	44.40	41.78	42.79

which is relatively similar to English, but are, in fact, of no use whatever in learning a language whose structure is quite different from that of English. To go one step further, the results obtained with the Vietnamese groups could be interpreted to mean that the training in English structure and sound-symbol relationship inhibited rather than facilitated the learning of Vietnamese.

While differential gains in aptitude were made by both Experimental and Control Groups, none of these differences was statistically significant. Table 2 summarizes the gains and differences in gains for all classes. It will be noted that the difference in gains for all languages combined favors the Control Groups, and that the greatest differences in gains for the individual languages (Arabic, Russian, and Vietnamese) were also made by the Control Groups. It will also be noted that the superior groups in Spanish and Vietnamese were also the ones that made the greatest gains among all classes.

Table 2 seems to indicate that there are obvious differences between the gains made by the different language groups. These differences, however, must be associated with the initial aptitude level of the groups. Those that started on the lower level made greater gains. Table 3 shows the ranking of the Experimental and Control Groups according to initial aptitude and gains in aptitude.

In order to check the possibility that the differences in gains were a reflection of the initial level of aptitude, the scores of the students within the top and bottom 25% of initial aptitude scores were examined in greater detail. Table 4 shows the pretest and post-test means for all classes combined and the gains made on the post-test.

TABLE 2

Gains and Differences in Gain in Aptitude

	Experimental	Control	Difference
Arabic	1.5	6.6	5.1
Chinese	6.9	5.2	1.7
Russian	4.7	8.8	4.1
Spanish	12.9	10.8	2.1
Vietnamese	7.8	11.4	3.6
All classes	7.0	8.7	1.7

TABLE 3

Rank Order of Classes in Initial Aptitude
and Aptitude Gain

Experimental Classes		Control Classes	
Initial Aptitude	Gain in Aptitude	Initial Aptitude	Gain in Aptitude
Arabic	Spanish	Arabic	Vietnamese
Chinese	Vietnamese	Chinese	Spanish
Russian	Chinese	Russian	Russian
Vietnamese	Russian	Vietnamese	Arabic
Spanish	Arabic	Spanish	Chinese

The "negative" gains in the top 25% are not entirely unexpected. Since high-aptitude students have already reached the upper limits of performance, small gains or even loss on the retest do not represent an unusual phenomenon. What is somewhat surprising is the magnitude of the loss in the Experimental Group (-2.54) as opposed to that of the Control Group (-1.12). Again, this suggests that the training may, in fact, have introduced inhibiting factors in conjunction with training in languages structurally dissimilar to English.

The aptitude training which took place must be interpreted as part of the *total training* which included the language course itself. In conjunction with a language, like Spanish, which shares certain structural features with English (e.g., significance of word order), training in English structure may have helped to increase certain aspects of aptitude, while the same training in conjunction with Russian, which is structurally quite different from English, may have inhibited certain factors connected with aptitude (e.g., flexibility in dealing with language structure).

A very crucial question concerning the interpretation of the

TABLE 4

Mean Scores and Gains for Army Language
Aptitude Test for First and Fourth
Quartiles, All Languages Combined

		Pre-test	Post-test	Gain
Top 25%	Experimental	47.04	44.50	-2.54
	Control	45.96	44.83	-1.12
Bottom 25%	Experimental	25.69	38.19	$+12.50$
	Control	24.96	36.21	$+11.25$

increase in aptitude shown by the retake of the test is, of course, to what extent these increases reflect only the fact that the students are repeating a test already taken. Fortunately, it was possible to arrange for a retake of the Army Aptitude Test by a group of subjects who were not exposed to any kind of language training between the two administrations of the test. Table 5 summarizes the mean scores of the Experimental and Control Groups and of the second Control Group on the first and second administration of the Language Aptitude Tests.

TABLE 5

Total Mean Scores and Gains on Pre-test
and Post-test of Army Language
Aptitude Battery

	Experimental	Control	Second Control
Pre-test	34.78	34.09	33.83
Post-test	41.78	42.79	38.35
Gains	7.00	8.70	4.52

The interval between the pre-test and the post-test was much smaller for this second Control Group than it was for either the first Control Group or the Experimental Group. In spite of the fact that this "recency effect" would be expected to favor the second Control Group, the students who took the post-test without intervening language training scored much lower than the students in the first Control Group, who had not been exposed to the Experimental materials but who had been exposed to language training. Thus, the obvious conclusion suggests itself that the most important aptitude training consisted in the intensive Army Course itself!

THE HIGH-SCHOOL EXPERIMENT

Table 6 summarizes the mean scores obtained in the high-school experiment. As can be inferred from an examination of this table, the high-school experiment was beset with various difficulties. Only three of the pairs of classes taking part in the experiment (Spanish Classes 1 and 2, German Classes 3 and 4, and Spanish Classes 13 and 14) furnished complete sets of all experimental data. Motivation (and,

TABLE 6

High-School Experiment: Summary of Mean Scores for A I Classes

	Spanish Class 1 Exper. (N=28)	Spanish Class 2 Control (N=28)	German Class 3 Exper. (N=23)	German Class 4 Control (N=25)	French Class 5 Exper. (N=28)	French Class 6 Control (N=23)	French Class 7 Exper. (N=31)	French Class 8 Control (N=30)	Spanish Class 9 Exper. (N=25)	Spanish Class 10 Control (N=25)	French Class 11 Exper. (N=17)	French Class 12 Control (N=14)	Spanish Class 13 Exper. (N=29)	Spanish Class 14 Control (N=29)
MLAT Pre-test	26.26	23.72	30.48	32.60	30.96	30.00	29.10	32.33	26.34	26.17	23.71	26.50	22.66	19.37
MLAT 2 Pre-test	20.47	19.44	22.04	23.16	21.64	21.23	21.79	21.42	21.23	19.50	11.78	19.50	18.31	18.69
MLAT 3 Pre-test	13.00	8.39	11.65	14.92	11.34	11.72	14.27	13.75	12.11	13.04	10.14	7.50	6.85	9.06
MLAT 4 Pre-test	13.42	13.03	14.04	16.52	16.84	13.94	19.33	15.48	14.50	11.45	14.42	15.07	10.50	10.10
MLAT 5 Pre-test	14.19	13.00	13.91	15.80	15.57	13.47	16.13	14.02	11.34	12.45	14.06	10.35	10.17	10.93
Auditory Discrim. 1	6.48		6.59		—*		—		—		6.41		6.47	
Auditory Discrim. 2	5.25		5.40		5.58		—		—		5.66		5.50	
Auditory Discrim. 3	5.39		0.42		—		—		—		—		6.00	
Sounds of English	11.95		14.75		13.21		12.56		12.52		8.42		9.37	
Structure of English	7.50		11.90		13.29		—		11.85		8.23		9.89	
MLAT 2 Post-test	22.73	20.87	24.35	23.27	—	—	—	22.25	23.45	22.13	—	—	21.37	20.09
MLAT 3 Post-test	15.13	13.75	17.41	17.95	—	—	—	21.89	11.50	17.08	—	—	10.87	9.54
MLAT 4 Post-test	16.13	17.70	17.76	17.86	—	—	—	17.56	17.81	16.56	—	—	14.12	11.45

*—indicates results not available.

as a result, achievement in experimental training) on the part of the students was rather low. There is also a distinct possibility that the experimental groups may have developed feelings of animosity toward the experiment and that these feelings may, to some extent, have depressed their scores on the tests. Although the Progress Tests which had been written for the experiment were administered to all students during the second semester (in January, March, and May), no discernible pattern seems to emerge from the obtained scores. Thus, the only scores reported in Table 7 are those obtained from the final Progress Test. (See pp. 11 and 12 for a description of the three parts of this test.)

TABLE 7

Mean Scores on Final Progress Tests

	Final Progress Part A	Final Progress Part B	Final Progress Part C
Spanish Class 1 (Exper., N=28)	5.35	6.80	7.75
Spanish Class 2 (Control, N=28)	7.82	8.83	9.43
German Class 3 (Exper., N=23)	6.93	6.75	10.75
German Class 4 (Control, N=25)	7.31	7.86	10.36
French Class 5 (Exper., N=28)	5.43	5.30	6.47
French Class 6 (Control, N=23)	4.76	4.35	5.76
French Class 7 (Exper., N=31)	—	—	—
French Class 8 (Control, N=30)	5.34	5.26	6.80
Spanish Class 9 (Exper., N=26)	7.00	9.19	10.14
Spanish Class 10 (Control, N=25)	6.00	7.52	8.21
French Class 11 (Exper., N=17)	4.36	3.00	4.73
French Class 12 (Control, N=14)	5.50	4.02	6.75
Spanish Class 13 (Exper., N=29)	6.31	6.00	6.19
Spanish Class 14 (Control, N=29)	8.00	5.86	6.87

Both the Experimental and the Control Groups showed gains in the retake of the aptitude tests (MLAT 2, 3, and 4). Table 8 summarizes the gains and the differences in gains of the total high-school Experimental and Control Groups.

TABLE 8

Gains and Differences in Gains on MLAT 2, 3, and 4
for All High-School Classes Combined

	Experimental	Control	Difference
MLAT 2	2.49	0.55	1.94
MLAT 3	2.86	5.45	2.59
MLAT 4	1.65	3.33	1.68

The results show that the Experimental Groups performed better than the Control Groups only on MLAT 2 (Phonetic Script), that part of the MLAT most directly connected with the training procedures. However, the greatest difference in gain occurred in MLAT 3 (Spelling Cues) in favor of the Control Groups! As stated earlier, it is difficult to assess to what extent motivational factors may have lowered the scores of the Experimental Groups on the aptitude retest. It is, however, quite conceivable that the training in Sound-Symbol relationship—and especially the emphasis on phonetic transcription—did, in fact, inhibit the performance on MLAT 3 which tests, to a large degree, flexibility in Sound-Symbol relationship. The concept of "one sound, one symbol" which is emphasized by training in phonetic or phonemic transcription is indeed quite apposed to the flexibility factor tested in MLAT 3. MLAT 2, as such (phonemic script), does not in any way contradict MLAT 3, that is, the ability to recognize phonemic transcription as an alternative way of representing sounds can be considered as another way of showing flexibility in Sound-Symbol relationship. Evidently, training in phonemic transcription does not contribute to such flexibility and may thus account for the lower performance of the Experimental Group on the retake of MLAT 3.

As with the Defense Language Institute experiment, test-retest gains in language aptitude were considered in the light of initial level of aptitude. The scores of the students in the upper and lower quartiles of initial aptitude scores were examined in greater detail. Table 9 summarizes the differences in gain between the first quartile and the fourth quartile. On all three tests (MLAT 2, 3, 4) the differences in gain were in favor of the lowest quartile.

TABLE 9

Differences in Gain in Aptitude Tests
Between Top 25% and Bottom 25%

	Experimental	Control
MLAT 2	1.75	3.96
MLAT 3	5.14	5.30
MLAT 4	1.72	5.79

The scores for the Experimental and Control Groups were considered in both the upper and the lower quartiles. Table 10 summarizes the results of these comparisons.

TABLE 10

Differences in Gain in Aptitude Tests
Between Experimental and
Control Groups

	Top 25%	Bottom 25%
MLAT 2	1.65*	.56
MLAT 3	4.42	4.58
MLAT 4	1.79*	1.28

*Difference in Gain in favor of Experimental Groups

Consideration of the gains made by the upper and lower 25% of the students does not change the picture of the superiority of the Control Group over the Experimental Group in MLAT 3. The fact that the greatest gain within the top 25% is the gain of the Control Groups on MLAT 3 (4.42) seems to confirm the suspicion that the experimental training did indeed inhibit rather than facilitate performance on that part of the test. What seems somewhat more puzzling is the evidence that within the lower 25% the Experimental Groups gained less than the Control Groups not only on MLAT 3 but also on MLAT 2 and 4, to which the aptitude training had quite specifically addressed itself. It seems unlikely, for example, that training in the Structure of English should have inhibited performance on MLAT 4, which is concerned with sensitivity to words in sentences, but this seems to have been the case. However, as was pointed out earlier, teachers and assistants connected with the experiment reported that students in the Experimental Groups resented the training program for various reasons (e.g., they found the training "too hard," "too time-consuming," "not related to the course," and so on). This resentment against the program may very well have depressed scores on tests connected with the training within the Experimental Groups—and it is only reasonable to assume that such resentment was most pronounced among the lower-aptitude students.

Since most of the students taking part in the high-school experiment were 9th graders, it was possible to compare their pre-test and post-test performances on MLAT 2, 3, and 4 with the fluctuations on total test scores indicated by Carroll and Sapon (Test Manual, p. 9) occurring between 9th, 10th, and 11th grades, separated by sex. Table 11 summarizes the data from the Carroll-Sapon report.

TABLE 11

Mean Scores on MLAT, Total Test
(Parts 1, 2, 3, 4, 5)

	Male		Female	
	Mean	Gain	Mean	Gain
9th Grade	87.7		89.2	
10th Grade	84.3	−3.8%	92.2	3.3%
11th Grade	90.7	7.5%	103.4	12.3%

Table 12 summarizes the Mean scores on the MLAT tests 2, 3, and 4 made by male and female subjects in the Experimental and Control Groups.

Of course, it is not quite accurate to compare the percentage gains which are reported by Carroll and Sapon for the test as a whole with those recorded by the experiment which concerns only MLAT 2, 3, and 4. Still, one can infer that the gains made by the participants in the experiment are very different from those occurring as a result of maturation. Thus, in the Carroll-Sapon sample, there is actually a drop of 3.8% in the scores of boys in the 10th grades compared with the 9th, and only a very slight gain (3.3%) in the girl group. All the groups participating in the experiments showed rather clear gains.

In the DLI experiment, the "second control" group showed a gain from 33.03 to 38.35, or of about 14%, merely a result of

TABLE 12

Mean Scores on MLAT 2, 3, and 4
Made by 9th Grade Students in
High-School Experiment

	Male			Female		
	Pre-test Mean	Post-test Mean	% of Gain	Pre-test Mean	Post-test Mean	% of Gain
Exper. Groups	44.36	52.18	17.5	47.06	54.98	16.8
Control Groups	45.09	51.36	13.9	46.84	60.96	30.1

familiarity with the tests. The Experimental and Control Groups showed gains of 34.78 to 41.78 (about 20%) and 34.09 to 42.79 (about 25%). Since the Army Language Aptitude tests and the MLAT tests are highly correlated (at levels from .80 to .91, see Adjutant General's Office, Dept. of the Army, Research Memorandum 59-3, 1959), the comparison in percentage gain in the scores of MLAT 2, 3, and 4 and the Army Language Tests in the DLI, allows at least some conjecture as to whether the gains on the retake of aptitude tests in the high school were largely due to familiarity with the test. It seems that, at least, the very high gain achieved by the girl control group (30.1%) cannot be accounted for by familiarity with the test alone.

In general, aptitude scores of boys and girls show a pattern of slightly higher scores for girls. Table 13 summarizes the pre-test and post-test scores on MLAT 2, 3, and 4 for the classes from which complete test results were available.

Thus it appears that in all cases, with the exception of MLAT 3 in the Experimental Groups, girls made greater gains than boys. However, even this exception may be more apparent than real. As we have pointed out earlier, we suspect that the training may actually have had an adverse effect on performance on MLAT 3. In other words, the results throughout appear to indicate that training is more effective with girls than with boys.

TABLE 13

Pre-test Means, Post-test Means, and Net Gains on MLAT 2, 3, and 4 for Classes from Which Complete Results Were Available

	MLAT 2			MLAT 3			MLAT 4		
	Pre-test	Post-test	Gains	Pre-test	Post-test	Gains	Pre-test	Post-test	Gains
Male									
Exper. Group (N=29)	20.91	22.90	1.99	11.07	13.90	2.83	12.38	15.38	3.00
Control Group (N=46)	20.31	21.12	.81	12.03	14.93	2.90	12.75	15.31	2.56
Female									
Exper. Group (N=40)	20.69	23.25	2.56	12.27	14.33	2.06	14.10	17.40	3.30
Control Group (N=30)	21.17	23.35	2.18	11.92	17.54	5.62	13.75	20.07	6.32

SUMMARY AND CONCLUSIONS

It seems that perhaps the most effective "aptitude training" received by any of the students taking part in the experiments reported was the intensive language training given by the Defense Language Institute. The rather short training in auditory discrimination, English structure, and so on in the aptitude training program is undoubtedly ineffective if compared with the many hours of auditory training and training in structure inherent in the intensive audio-lingual Defense Language Institute courses. At any rate, the only clear gain in aptitude scores was registered by both the Defense Language Institute Experimental and Control Groups over a comparable group that had received no language training.

There also seems to be some evidence that the first year of audio-lingual training in high school may by itself constitute some aptitude training. This suggestion does not necessarily imply that additional training in the same language or training in other languages would lead to further increases in aptitude, nor does it contradict the recent findings of T. G. Sturgis (Sturgis, 1967) who showed that success in learning an African language was related to aptitude, but not to the amount of foreign-language study undertaken in high school.

There is some indication that the kind of aptitude training emphasized in the experiment which was primarily related to English Structure and to English Sound-Symbol Relationship (phonemic transcription) may be effective only with languages which have some structural similarity to English. Training in the Structure of English may, in fact, have an adverse effect on learning languages which are structurally radically different from English. In the Defense Language Institute experiment, for instance, the Vietnamese Experimental Group ranked substantially lower than the Control Group on at least one of the final criterion measures.

The concept that training in the skills to be tested in the various parts of the MLAT may, in fact, have an inhibiting influence on some language skills or the learning of some languages does not necessarily contradict the contention and the fact that the Carroll-Sapon test predicts equally well for all languages (see Carroll-Sapon Test Manual, p. 21). The *ability* to grasp quickly sound-symbol relationships as presented by phonemic transcription (tested in MLAT, part 2) is not to be confused with the possible effects of prolonged *training* in phonemic transcription. The former measures flexibility in the recognition of sound-symbol relations while the latter may simply emphasize a rigid sound-symbol concept. At any rate, the experiment gave some indication that the experimental training had an adverse effect on the flexibility implied in the recognition of sound-symbol relations measured in MLAT 3. The training in English structure may be in a similar relation to the skills measured in MLAT 4 (sensitivity to recognition of the structural function of English words in sentences) as the training in phonemic transcription is to the skills measured in MLAT 3. The *ability* to recognize the structural function of words in the English sentence correlates highly with the ability to recognize structural relations in other languages, but there is some indication that *training* in English structure induces a certain rigidity (an expectation that other languages should behave like English) especially among students who are initially of lower aptitude.

The experiments, thus, indicated various factors that would have to be considered in any attempt to increase language aptitude by specific training:

a) Careful distinctions should be made between skills associated with language aptitude and the possible effects of training to develop these skills.

b) If the training program is designed to increase general aptitude (and not merely achievement in a specific language), then it must avoid giving training in specific skills associated with only one particular language or type of language.

c) The possible effect achieved by the training undertaken in the last part of the program (Inductive Learning Ability) had to be further explored. This training (50 frames of Japanese structure) constituted only a very small part of the training program, and its effects were not considered in any of the post-tests or criterion measures.

d) Finally, the effectiveness of the training program as a whole had to be increased. First of all, the program would have to be commensurate with the initial level of aptitude of the students. The program used in this phase of the experiment seemed to be comparatively easy for the students in the Defense Language Institute, but much too difficult for the high-school students. While the Defense Language Institute students, by and large, had no trouble reaching criterion measures, few high-school students performed satisfactorily on the tests measuring success in the program.

Secondly, certain indications of low motivation such as lack of interest on the part of participating students, resentment of the training program, incompleted criterion tests, and so on, had to be eliminated from the training procedures if the experiment were to be effective.

These points were taken into consideration in the design and execution of Phase II of the experiment.

Phase II of the Experiment

PROCEDURE

EXPERIMENTAL DESIGN

The design of Phase II of the experiment and the materials developed for it were based on the conclusions derived from Phase I. The basic design followed the Pre-test, Post-test Exprimental-Control Group model with the exception that the Control Group was given a particular treatment at the same time and of the same duration as the Experimental Group. Six teachers, two in German, two in French, and two in Spanish, each one teaching at least two first-year junior-high-school foreign-language classes, were recruited from 3 schools in the San Francisco Bay area to participate in the study. Two classes were selected at random for each teacher, and the Experimental and Control Groups were randomly assigned from these. The Experimental Groups received the training for approximately ten minutes two or three times a week during their regular foreign-language class sessions. On the same days, the Control Groups were given specially prepared cultural materials. The entire training program lasted eleven weeks. In order to equalize the "Hawthorne Effect," both Experimental and Control Groups were told that they were participating in an experiment designed to measure the effects of specially prepared extra-curricular materials on classroom learning. In reality, there was some expectation that the treatment given to the Control Groups was more than a placebo. Since motivation is such an important factor in language learning, it is quite possible that an interesting exposure to the cultural aspects of the country whose language was being studied could generate or increase motivation, the effects of which would be apparent in an increase in language achievement.

TRAINING PROGRAM

The rationale and procedures for the development and administration of the training program were based on the conclusions derived from Phase I of the experiment, namely, that the material to be developed should be appropriate to high-school or junior-high-school level; that the materials should emphasize inductive learning ability rather than training in a specific language; that steps should be taken to generate and maintain interest and motivation throughout the program on the part of both teachers and students.

The most obvious and direct means of insuring interest and motivation would appear to be through the teachers themselves. It seems reasonable to assume that teachers involved in the actual development and writing of the program as well as in its administration would be more interested in the experiment and would in turn pass this interest on to their students. With this in mind, it was arranged that the six teachers whose classes were to participate in the experiment be hired for the summer as part-time research assistants at one-sixth salary per teacher. Writing of the experimental materials was begun in June, at the end of the school year, and continued on throughout the summer. The teachers worked in pairs in collaboration with the assistant investigator, and the entire group met from time to time with the principal investigator to review and evaluate the work.

Due to the fact that the Stanford Secondary Teacher Education Program (STEP) was in progress at this time, it was possible to pre-test the experimental material as it was being written. The material was administered to a group of fifteen of the high-school students participating in the STEP program, analyzed for reliability and level of difficulty, rewritten by the assistant investigator, and administered again to another group of students.

During this period, the teachers also developed the cultural lessons that were to be used with the Control Groups. The teachers worked in pairs in their respective language areas and wrote twenty-three short essays about various aspects of the life and language of the people of Mexico, France, and Germany. Although no tests were constructed for these materials, most of the essays were followed by short quizzes.

The experimental aptitude training material consisted of twenty-three lessons, divided into two parts, as follows:

Part 1: Short-term Memory Training

This part of the program was based primarily on two of the factors involved in language aptitude as identified by Carroll (see p. 2 of this report), namely, phonetic coding and rote memory. The first six lessons which comprise Part I of the training program were presented on audio-tape and were devoted to practice in listening, repetition, and information retrieval. In the early stages of audio-lingual language study, students are required to remember sequences of strange sounds, to repeat them and, in the case of substitution drills, to locate the element of the sentence that is to be replaced. It is perhaps awareness of the importance of these processes rather than mere repetition and practice which can improve the students' ability in the early stages of language learning. It was thus the intent of this part of the training program to point up the importance of attending to and repeating sequences of unfamiliar sounds.

The first three lessons introduced the student to these two elementary aspects of remembering: careful listening and repetition. The student was presented with strings of numbers or nonsense syllables, told to listen carefully, to repeat the stimuli and then to identify them from the answer sheet or to write the numbers in the correct sequence.

The next three lessons introduced the student to a number code in which numbers 1 through 5 represented five different sounds, as follows: $1 = k$; $2 = æ$; $3 = č$; $4 = i$; $5 = s$. Sequences of these sounds were arranged in such a way as to avoid any combination occurring in English. These sequences were presented in strings of increasing length and the student was required to write the numbers corresponding to the sounds. In some exercises, the student was required to select a specific string of sounds from among three sets of numeric symbols, while in others the task consisted in identifying one of three strings presented on the tape which corresponded to a set of numeric symbols on the answer sheet. A progress test at the end of the sixth lesson required the student to perform the same type of task.

Part 2: Grammatical Sensitivity and Inductive Learning

Seventeen lessons designed primarily to train the student in the inductive learning ability comprised the second part of the training program. These lessons, like the first six, were written in the form of an instructional program with the correct responses for each frame given at the beginning of the following frame.

In order to keep the training general rather than specific to any one language, several artificial languages were devised for the training materials. This variety in languages was intended to encourage the flexibility of the student's approach to language learning. In some cases, the student was given examples of certain grammatical principles and was asked to write new forms in the artificial language or to choose a correct form from among several alternatives. In other cases, the student was required to select from among several alternatives an explanation to account for certain grammatical constructions. Several times throughout the lessons a deliberately uncertain response (e.g., "There is no way of knowing yet") was used to encourage the student to look for further information before making a decision. As a vehicle for these tasks, the lessons presented the student with the grammatical concepts of number, tense, and case, arranged in levels of increasing complexity. The tasks required of the student were quite similar to those involved in Part 4 (Language Analysis) of the Pimsleur Language Aptitude Battery.

CRITERION MEASURES

There were three main types of criterion measures used in this phase of the experiment: one related to the specific aptitudes involved in the training program, one related to achievement in the specific languages the students were learning and one, the Pimsleur LAB, related to language aptitude in general. The Pimsleur LAB was administered in the first week of the school year to all students participating in the study, and scores on this test were used later to adjust the class means of all other tests. The training program Progress Test was administered to both the Experimental and Control Groups several days after the completion of the training and was followed one week later by the Pimsleur LAB Post test. Since it was not possible to obtain grade point averages for students coming from 6th grade into 7th grade, and since Parts 1 (Grade Point Average) and 2 (Attitude to Language Study) do not measure aptitude as such, only parts 3, 4, 5, and 6 of this test were used. Scores on these tests were used to investigate the first problem posed by the experiment: "Is it possible to increase language aptitude through specific training?" Since there is at the present time no alternate form of the Pimsleur LAB, there is a possibility that a re-test of the same items after such a short period of time might serve to raise the class means simply through familiarity with the material. This possibility will be discussed later in the report. The Language Achievement Tests, written specifically for German, French, and Spanish, were given in January and in May and were designed to investigate the second problem posed by the experiment: "Does an increase in aptitude brought about through specific training truly reflect a higher learning ability as measured by success in foreign-language study?"

Following is a brief description of the criterion measures written especially for the experiment:

Progress Test

This test was given to all students several days after the completion of the training program. The test was designed to measure the aptitudes involved in the experimental training but was independent of the material used in the training program itself.

The first part of the test (Listening) presented the student with the task of retrieving certain information from strings of words previously recorded on audio-tape. The maximum score on this test was seven. It was expected that students who had been trained to listen carefully and repeat after the model would perform better than students in the Control Groups.

The second part of the test (Grammar) presented morphological problems from three languages: Swahili, Samoan, and Maori. Cues were presented in such a way as to permit students in the Control Groups, who had not had specific training in grammatical sensitivity, to solve the problems. It was expected, however, that the students in the Experimental Groups would perform better than those in the Control Groups. The maximum score for this test was fifteen. An analysis of the items on this test and application of the Kuder-Richardson Formula 20 yielded a reliability coefficient of .81.

Language Achievement Tests

The first Language Achievement Test was given to all students in January, approximately six weeks after the completion of the training program. Although the tests were specific to German, French, and Spanish, the problems, format, and maximum scores were approximately the same for all languages. The test consisted of the following four parts:

Completion Test.—In this test, the stem of each item contained a missing word. The student was given two words and was required to designate whether the first word, the second word, both words, or neither could be used to complete the sentence. The maximum score on this test was 20.

Substitution Test.—In this test, the stem of each item contained an underlined word. The task was the same as in the Completion Test with the exception that the student was required to designate the substitution of the underlined word rather than the completion of the sentence. The maximum score on this test was 15.

Grammar Test.—In this test, the student was required to change sentences from plural to singular in Spanish and French and to make changes in case in German. The maximum score on this test was 17.

Reading Test.—In this test, the student was required to read a paragraph containing seven missing words and find the correct words from among a list of fourteen, seven of which were distractors. The maximum score on this test was 7.

The Final Language Achievement Test was given during the second week in May, and was somewhat shorter than the first Achievement Test. In the first part of the test, the student was required to rewrite a number of sentences from the singular to the plural and, in the case of German, to replace a number of nouns with pronouns. In the second part of the test, the student was presented with a narrative of approximately 100 words. The story was narrated in the third person, and the task of the student was to retell the story in the first person, making all necessary changes in pronouns, verbs, possessive adjectives, and so forth. The total score on this test was 25 for French, 28 for German, and 26 for Spanish.

The following data were obtained for all classes participating in Phase II of the experiment:

Pimsleur LAB (Pre-test)	Administered in September
Training Program	Administered in November
Progress Test, Listening	
Progress Test, Grammar	
Pimsleur LAB (Post-test)	Administered in December
Language Achievement Test	Administered in January
Substitution Test	
Completion Test	
Grammar Test	
Reading Test	
Final Achievement Test	Administered in May

Appendix II shows the correlations of the Pimsleur Tests with the Experimental Criterion Measures. Although none of the correlation coefficients is above .50, the number of students involved insures rather high levels of significance. Thus, it could be said that most of the criterion tests are closely enough related to language aptitude as measured by the LAB to warrant their use.

All materials developed for both Phase I and Phase II of the experiment are available for examination and use upon request. A complete list of this material will be found in Appendix I.

STUDENT ATTITUDE MEASURES

The question of student attitude toward the training program and its effect on test performance was an important one in Phase I of the experiment, and measures had been taken to increase interest and motivation in the second phase. Teachers had been recruited to participate in the development of the materials, the training material had been shortened and simplified, and the lessons had been distributed one at a time on alternate days during the class period, so that no homework was required of the student. Teachers had been asked to remind their students frequently that the materials (the training program in the case of the Experimental Groups and the culture program in the case of the Control Groups) were designed to increase their achievment in the language they were studying.

At the completion of the training program, students in both the Control Groups and Experimental Groups were asked to complete a short attitude questionnaire, expressing their opinions about the training program (see Appendix III). The questionnaire contained five statements, followed by a choice of three responses: agree, no opinion, and disagree. A positive opinion was given a value of three points, a neutral opinion a value of two points, and a negative opinion a value of one point. One statement ("I thought the material was too easy") was included for its feedback value to the investigators and teachers and was not included in the attitude score. Thus, the maximum score on this scale was 12. Table 14 summarizes the means and standard deviations for all classes and the "t" values for the differences between the Experimental and Control Groups for each teacher. Obviously, the attitude of students in the Control Groups was toward the cultural materials and not the training program, and a more favorable opinion on the part of the Control Groups is to be expected. Nevertheless, the differences in favor of the Control Groups are great enough to warrant consideration in respect to the effect on scores in the Progress Test and the Language Achievement Tests.

TABLE 14

Attitude of Students to Experiment

	Experimental Classes			Control Classes			t
	Mean	sd	N	Mean	sd	N	
Teacher #1 (French)	8.21	2.12	25	9.73	2.05	17	2.26*
Teacher #2 (French)	7.80	2.46	25	8.76	2.35	25	1.38
Teacher #3 (German)	9.25	2.69	22	11.14	1.12	24	3.09**
Teacher #4 (German)	7.21	2.71	24	10.35	2.06	20	4.16**
Teacher #5 (Spanish)	7.38	2.74	18	10.11	1.20	10	3.70**
Teacher #6 (Spanish)	7.94	2.46	23	10.60	1.66	21	4.07**

*p < .05
**p < .01

It is quite possible that, in spite of the steps that were taken to increase interest and motivation, the same type of resentment toward extra-curricular language work that was evident in Phase I is also in evidence in this phase of the experiment and that this resentment would operate to depress the scores of the Experimental Groups on the criterion tests. On the other hand, it is possible that the cultural materials, which were of great interest to the teachers themselves, would generate enough interest in the language to contribute to an increase in scores on the criterion tests.

SECOND CONTROL GROUPS

There are two important points to be taken into consideration in determining the effectiveness of specific training on increase in language aptitude. One point is concerned with the re-test effect on post-test scores. The other point is raised by the fact that the training program was conducted concurrently with normal foreign-language study. We would expect normal foreign-language study to affect not only the scores on the language achievement tests but also the scores on the Pimsleur Language Aptitude Battery post-test. Indeed, as was pointed out in the discussion of Phase I of the experiment, the intensive language courses of the Defense Language Institute accounted for the only impressive increase in language aptitude. Although an analysis of covariance was used to determine the differential effects of treatment and normal foreign-language study in this phase of the experiment, the question still remained concerning the effectiveness of the training program on the aptitude of students not concurrently studying any foreign language.

Since foreign-language study is mandatory in the school district in which the experiment was conducted, it was difficult to find students who were not enrolled in foreign-language classes. Fortunately, it was possible to recruit four so-called "study skills" classes of seventh-grade students not engaged in foreign-language study. These classes were composed of students who were exempt, for one reason or another (usually because of low scores on general aptitude tests or low grades in elementary school English), from the school district's mandatory language requirement. Work done in these study-skills classes ranged from remedial reading and vocabulary study in English to a brief introductory exposure to Latin (in two of the classes). Although these classes could, therefore, not be assumed to be completely free of any language training, they were used as a "Second Control Group" to test the prediction that exposure to the experimental training program with no concurrent foreign-language study would raise the aptitude scores of these students.

During the spring semester, three study-skills classes were given the Pimsleur LAB, followed by Part 2 (Grammatical Sensitivity)only of the training program. Part 1 (Listening) was not given, since it seemed, for reasons to be discussed later, to be ineffective with the classes in the main part of the experiment. At the end of the training period, the three classes were given the Grammar component of the Aptitude Training Progress Test as well as the post-test of the Pimsleur LAB. As in the main part of Phase II, only the last four components of the LAB were given. The results obtained from these Second Control Groups will be discussed in the following section of this report.

A fourth study-skills class was used to investigate the re-test effect on post-test scores on the Pimsleur LAB. This class was given the LAB in February and again in April after an interval of eight weeks. Other than the normal vocabulary and remedial reading work in English, no treatment was given to this class. The unadjusted means for the pre-test and post-test of Parts 3, 4, 5, and 6 of the LAB are as follows:

Pre-test Mean: 33.80

Post-test Mean: 36.62

Thus, it can be observed that the gain score for this class after an interval of eight weeks was 2.82 points. Although no conclusions could be drawn from a sample of only one class, it is of interest to note that under the direction of Dr. Harold F. Bligh, Test Department, Harcourt, Brace and World, Inc., a study was conducted in the spring of 1966 in which 6th- and 8th-grade students (in Massachusetts and New Jersey) took the LAB twice within a period of ten days in order to supply data for the establishment of Test-Retest Reliability Coefficients. Through personal communication from Harcourt, Brace and World, Inc., the scores on these tests were supplied. Table

TABLE 15

Class Means and Gain Scores on Pimsleur LAB
(Test-retest)

Grade Level	N	Pre-test Mean	Post-test Mean	Gain Score
6	238	63.18	66.78	3.60
6	202	55.58	58.54	2.96
8	201	65.70	68.63	2.93
8	235	67.74	71.30	3.56

15 shows the means and gain scores for the pre-test and post-test for these classes. It should be kept in mind that the post-test was given after an interval of ten days and that the figures represent scores on the total test, that is, with Parts 1 and 2 included.

If we consider that neither Grade Point Average (Part 1) nor Interest in Foreign-Language Study (Part 2) would be likely to vary after ten days, it could be said that from available samples of test-retest scores a gain in aptitude of something like three points might be expected.

RESULTS AND DISCUSSION

Since increase in Language Aptitude is the main point of interest in this experiment, results of the Pimsleur LAB pre-test and post-test will be discussed first, followed by a discussion of the results of the Aptitude Training Progress Test. Finally, results of the Language Achievement Test given in January and the Final Language Achievement Test given in May will be discussed.

PIMSLEUR LANGUAGE APTITUDE BATTERY (LAB) POST-TEST

The statistical procedure used to analyze the data was a four-way analysis of covariance. The four variables were: Language, Teacher-within-Language, Treatment, and Sex. The covariate was the total score for Parts 3, 4, 5, and 6 of the Pimsleur LAB pre-test. The adjusted means for male and female subjects, arranged by language, class, and treatment groups were inspected for the contribution of each of these variables to the total variance between means and for the effects of the interaction of these variables. (Appendix Va summarizes the relevant aspects of the analysis of covariance.) The mean scores for all classes were adjusted according to the following formula:

$$\text{Adjusted score} = \overline{Y}_i - b_p (\overline{X}_i - \overline{X}_c)$$

in which

$\overline{Y}_i$ = raw score

b_p = regression slope for the pooled equation
for the variable

$\overline{X}_i$ = LAB mean score for the individual class

$\overline{X}_c$ = LAB combined mean score

An analysis of the regression of the scores for variable Y on the scores for variable X provided the combined mean score for X,

TABLE 16

Pimsleur Language Aptitude Battery: Unadjusted Means, Standard Deviations and Gain Scores

		Experimental Classes				Control Classes			
		Mean	sd	Gain	N	Mean	sd	Gain	N
Teacher #1 (French)	Pre-test	49.84	10.9	9.56	25	54.47	11.0	7.73	15
	Post-test	59.40	11.5			62.20	14.1		
Teacher #2 (French)	Pre-test	50.96	9.2	6.74	23	53.83	10.2	5.27	23
	Post-test	57.70	7.6			59.10	10.3		
Teacher #3 (German)	Pre-test	50.91	9.0	8.27	22	49.50	9.8	7.75	24
	Post-test	59.18	8.7			57.25	9.1		
Teacher #4 (German)	Pre-test	50.65	10.4	11.65	20	48.14	8.7	7.72	22
	Post-test	62.30	8.9			55.41	11.6		
Teacher #5 (Spanish)	Pre-test	47.22	9.3	5.44	18	49.17	7.0	6.22	18
	Post-test	52.67	10.6			55.39	8.6		
Teacher #6 (Spanish)	Pre-test	48.74	13.6	3.71	23	44.33	6.5	-.53	21
	Post-test	52.48	11.5			45.86	6.9		
Teacher #7 (Study Skills)	Pre-test	37.00	9.2	8.00	14	33.80	7.1	2.82*	16
	Post-test	45.00	6.4			36.62	9.9		
Teacher #8 (Study Skills)	Pre-test	42.86	6.4	9.35	14				
	Post-test	52.21	9.4						
Teacher #9 (Study Skills)	Pre-test	43.93	8.1	6.84	18				
	Post-test	50.78	9.4						

*Scores for this class represent the test-retest effect only, with no intervening language or treatment (see p. 37).

the regression slope for the pooled equation for the variable Y, the correlation coefficient for each class, and the F-ratio obtained from the test of parallelism of regression.

For the Pimsleur LAB, the following figures were obtained:

$$b_p = .75$$
$$\overline{X}_c = 49.75$$
$$r = .74$$
$$F = 1.35$$

Before discussing the adjusted mean scores, we might look at the unadjusted class means and the gain scores for all classes participating in Phase II of the experiment. Table 16 summarizes these data. What is of interest here are the gains made by classes 7, 8, and 9 (the study-skills classes with no concurrent foreign-language exposure) in relation to the other classes.

In the analysis of covariance, the F-ratio is obtained by dividing the variance that may be expected by chance into the variance obtained between two or more means. In the analysis of the Pimsleur LAB post-test, the highest F-ratio (12.6, significant at the .01 level) was obtained between the means of all French, all German, and all Spanish classes. The F-ratio obtained between the means of individual classes was 2.62, significant at the .05 level. The F-ratio obtained between the means of all the Experimental Groups and all the Control Groups was .20 (not significant), and the F-ratio for means of all male subjects and all female subjects was .08 (not significant). Thus, the greatest contribution to the differences in means was made by the three languages, the next greatest by the effects of the teachers, and no discernible contribution by either sex or treatment. The only other significant contribution to the systematic variance of the means was the interaction of teacher, treatment, and sex (F = 2.9, significant at the .05 level). Somewhat surprisingly and interestingly, the interaction between treatment and sex also approached significance: males in the Experimental Groups achieved definitely better than males in the Control Groups or females in either of the two groups. Figures la through le summarize these data.

Figure 1a.–Pimsleur LAB Post-test: Difference in Means
Between Experimental and Control Groups.

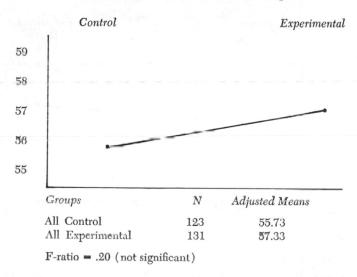

Groups	N	Adjusted Means
All Control	123	55.73
All Experimental	131	57.33

F-ratio = .20 (not significant)

In the discussion and interpretation of graphs 1a through 1c,
the reader should keep in mind that they attempt to represent
visually the differences between Experimental and Control
Groups as well as the differences due to language, teacher, and
sex. The differences between Experimental and Control Groups
correspond, of course, to the differences between the points on
the left (Control Groups) and right side (Experimental Groups)
of the graphs. In order to facilitate the reading of the graphs,
these points were connected by straight lines. The slope of the
lines indicates differences due to the treatments. The differences which are due to factors other than treatment can be
gleaned from the distances which exist along the vertical dimension between points on either the left or right side.

Figure 1a.–As the figure indicates, the Experimental Group
did, in fact, achieve somewhat better in the Pimsleur LAB post-
test than the Control Group. However, the difference between
the two means (55.73 vs. 55.33) is not statistically significant.

Figure 1b.–The slight superiority of the Experimental Groups
over the Control Groups shown in Figure 1a above exists also
within each language. However, there are obvious and significant (at the .01 level!) differences in the adjusted LAB scores

Figure 1b.—Pimsleur LAB Post-test: Differences in Means
Among French, German, and Spanish Classes.

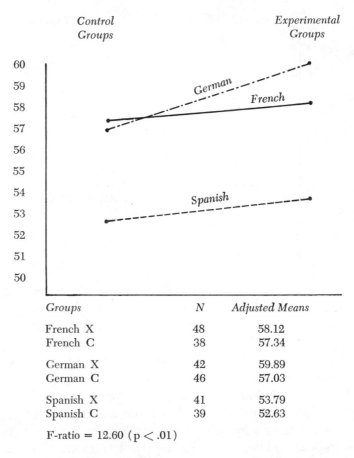

Groups	N	Adjusted Means
French X	48	58.12
French C	38	57.34
German X	42	59.89
German C	46	57.03
Spanish X	41	53.79
Spanish C	39	52.63

F-ratio = 12.60 $(p < .01)$

due to the language studied by the subjects. As can be seen
quite clearly from the graph, the differences between the German and French scores is negligible, but the significance in
difference is due entirely to the fact that the LAB scores of the
students in the Spanish classes lag far behind those of the German and French groups. It should be repeated here again that
the scores being compared in the graphs have already been
adjusted for initial aptitude differences. Thus, the lower performance of the students in the Spanish classes do not directly
reflect lower initial aptitude but rather the smaller gains made
by them. The interpretation of these obviously and significantly

Figure 1c.—Pimsleur LAB Post-test: Differences in
Means Among All Classes.

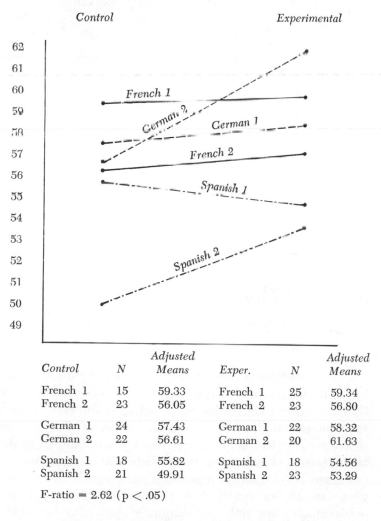

Control	N	Adjusted Means	Exper.	N	Adjusted Means
French 1	15	59.33	French 1	25	59.34
French 2	23	56.05	French 2	23	56.80
German 1	24	57.43	German 1	22	58.32
German 2	22	56.61	German 2	20	61.63
Spanish 1	18	55.82	Spanish 1	18	54.56
Spanish 2	21	49.91	Spanish 2	23	53.29

F-ratio = 2.62 (p < .05)

lower gains is difficult. It is, of course, rather tempting to specu-
late about the possibility that initial instruction in Spanish may
make less of a contribution to the increase of language aptitude
than instruction in French and German—perhaps because of the
relatively less complex grammar and sound-symbol relationship
problems met during the first few months of Spanish. However, there is also the possibility that the students in the Span-

Figure 1d.—Pimsleur LAB Post-test: Difference in
Means Between Combined Foreign-Language
Classes and Combined Study-Skills Classes.

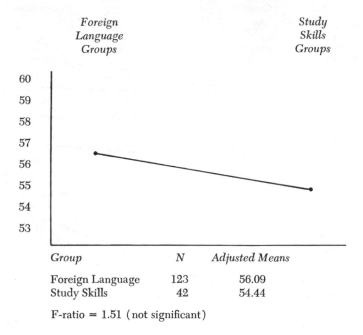

Group	N	Adjusted Means
Foreign Language	123	56.09
Study Skills	42	54.44

F-ratio = 1.51 (not significant)

ish classes were not only of lower initial aptitude but also that this initially lower aptitude was connected with lower motivation toward any kind of language achievement task. Whether or to what extent the lower aptitude scores of the Spanish students are due to the language they are studying or to motivational factors is impossible to assess in any concrete way.

Figure 1c.—Figure 1c repeats to some extent the information given in 1b, except that it shows the differences in LAB achievement not only by language but also by individual classes. The reader should keep in mind that French 1, French 2, etc., refer to pairs of classes (Experimental and Control) taught by the same teacher. The graph indicates again that the significance (p < .05) of difference in achievement on the LAB between classes is largely due to the lower performance of the Spanish classes. Spanish 1, incidentally, is the only one of the six pairs of classes in which the Control Group achieved higher

Figure 1e.—Pimsleur LAB Post-test: Difference in Means
Between Control and Experimental Groups by Sex   .

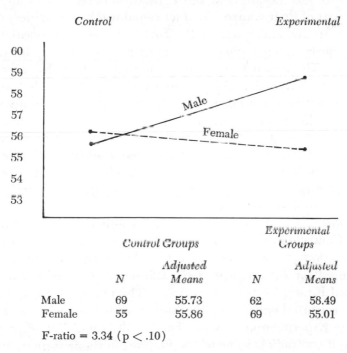

	Control Groups		Experimental Groups	
	N	Adjusted Means	N	Adjusted Means
Male	69	55.73	62	58.49
Female	55	55.86	69	55.01

F-ratio = 3.34 (p < .10)

than the Experimental Group. The highest gains of an Experimental Group over a Control Group occurred in German 1.

Figure 1d.—The comparison of the adjusted LAB means of the Study-Skills classes and the Foreign-Language classes involved in the experiment showed that the Foreign-Language classes achieved somewhat better, but that the difference between the groups was not significant. Thus, aptitude training combined with language training produced a LAB score of 57.33 (see 1a above), language training without aptitude training resulted in a score of 55.73 (see 1a above), and aptitude training without language training gave a result of 54.44. None of these differences is significant. One can conjecture that perhaps motivational factors tended to reduce differences in the LAB scores of these three groups. The "Foreign-Language and Aptitude Training" group was probably the least motivated to achieve on the LAB retake since the aptitude training had undoubtedly provoked some antagonistic reaction. The Study-

Skills group was quite likely the most motivated group since the aptitude training and the LAB were perceived as an integral part of their course. The fact remains that the achievement of the Study-Skills group on the LAB post-test was considerable (obviously much higher than could be ascribed to the retest effect). The lesson to be learned is that perhaps for no other reason than the effects of student motivation, aptitude training should not be undertaken once the student is already involved in a specific foreign-language course. On the other hand, the results achieved on the aptitude test by the "second control groups" of the experiment indicate that students with low language aptitude scores would most likely profit considerably from aptitude training given to them before they enroll in a specific foreign-language course.

Figure 1e.—The comparison of Experimental (Treatment) and Control Groups by sex gives a rather surprising result. The interaction of Treatment and Sex almost reaches the F-ratio required for significance at the .05 level (F-ratio = 3.34; required F-ratio for $p < .05$ is 3.60). The nearly significant variance is caused entirely by the higher achievement of the males in the Experimental Groups. This result is puzzling, especially since it contradicts some of the findings in the first phase of the experiment which seemed to indicate that females were perhaps more trainable than males. Did the experimental training devised for the second phase—dealing with induction of grammatical patterns and exotic languages—have more of a "masculine appeal" than the materials used in Phase I (e.g., English Grammar, sound-symbol correspondence in English), or were the males less antagonized than the females by being engaged in an activity that "took them away" from language learning as such? Unfortunately, none of these questions can be answered on the basis of the available data. The Attitude Questionnaire, since is was anonymous, can give us no clues as to the differential attitudes of the male and female subjects.

It is also quite possible that some of the teachers interacted more favorably with the boys than with the girls and this, in conjunction with the possibilities mentioned above, could have contributed to the difference. To investigate this possibility, Table 17 shows the adjusted mean scores for all classes

TABLE 17

Pimsleur Language Aptitude Battery Post-test:
Adjusted Means, Male and Female Control
and Experimental Groups

	Female		Male	
	Control	Experimental	Control	Experimental
French 1	58.33	59.84	59.75	57.99
French 2	57.89	50.03	54.29	57.56
German 1	54.77	58.21	58.97	58.57
German 2	50.61	54.49	55.69	64.87
Spanish 1	55.91	54.45	56.00	54.85
Spanish 2	49.62	52.54	50.46	54.37

according to sex. It will be noted that in German 2 and in Spanish 2 the boys in the Experimental Groups did better than any of the three other groups, while in French 2 and German 1 the boys in the Experimental Groups did as well as or better than the other three groups.

APTITUDE TRAINING PROGRESS TEST

The second set of criterion measures used in the experiment attempted to measure rather directly the progress and learning achieved by the experimental training itself and consisted of a listening test as well as a test measuring grammatical inductive ability. Just as in the case of the Pimsleur LAB post-test, the analysis of the data was carried out by means of an analysis of covariance applied to scores which had been adjusted for differences in initial language aptitude (LAB pre-test). In the regression analysis, the scores for the Listening Test and the scores for the Grammar Test were regressed separately on the Pimsleur LAB pre-test scores, and the following figures were obtained:

Listening	*Grammar*
$b_p = .03$	$b_p = .14$
$\overline{X}_c = 49.80$	$\overline{X}_c = 49.91$
$r = .22$	$r = .45$
$F = 1.10$	$F = .60$

The same procedures were carried out for the three Study-Skills classes and the Experimental classes of the six original

teachers. In this case, the aptitude training was held constant
while the independent variable in question was exposure or
non-exposure to foreign-language study. From the regression
analysis, the following figures were obtained:

$$b_p = .14$$
$$\overline{X}_c = 48.00$$
$$r = .34$$
$$F = .03$$

Although the unadjusted scores on this test will not be discussed here, Appendix IV summarizes the means and standard
deviations for all classes on both the Listening and the Grammar Tests. The relevent aspects of the analysis of covariance
for the Listening Test and the Grammar Test are summarized
in Appendices Vb and Vc.

The Experimental Groups did, by and large, perform somewhat better than the Control Groups, as should be expected
since the test was quite closely geared to the experimental
training. Rather disappointingly, the differences in performance between Experimental and Control Groups did not reach
significance level. This in turn may indicate that the training
was perhaps not as effective as it might have been or that, at
least, negative motivation in the Experimental Groups depressed performance on the progress test. The latter suspicion
appears to be justified by at least one rather surprising result:
the Second Control Group (the Study-Skills classes) outper-
formed the foreign-language classes (Experimental and Control Groups) on the Grammar component of the progress test
(adjusted means 11.9 as opposed to 9.48; $p < .01$!) in spite of
the fact that neither their initial nor their post-training aptitude
scores quite reached the level of the foreign-language classes.
Again, the results indicate that both the effectiveness of the
training and achievement in tests connected with the training
are heavily influenced by the way in which the training is perceived—as an unnecessary adjunct to an on-going language program or as an integral part of a learning experience in "study
skills."

The detailed results of the analysis of covariance are again presented with the help of a series of graphs. Figures 2a through 2d present the analysis of the Listening Test scores. The only significant F-ratio for this test was obtained between the means for all male and all female subjects regardless of training, and there is a possibility that this highly significant ratio ($F = 16.83$, p < .01) is unrelated to the training. It will be remembered that the training in listening skills was extremely short (only six lessons) and evidently not intensive enough for the Experimental Groups to achieve any real progress. The Listening Test itself was short and seemed to have only a slight relationship to the other measures in the experiment.

Figure 2a.—The difference in performance between the Experimental and Control Groups (.04 in favor of the Experimental Group) is negligible and obviously non-significant.

Figure 2b.—Note that in the German and Spanish classes the Control Groups outperform the Experimental Groups by a rather slim margin and that the differences in achievement due to language do not reach significance.

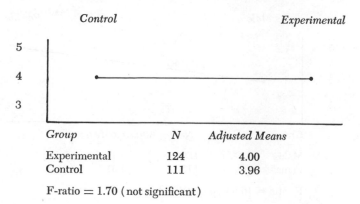

Figure 2a.—Progress Test—Listening: Difference in Means
Between Experimental and Control Groups.

Group	N	Adjusted Means
Experimental	124	4.00
Control	111	3.96

F-ratio = 1.70 (not significant)

Figure 2b. Progress Test—Listening: Differences in Means
Among French, German, and Spanish Claesses.

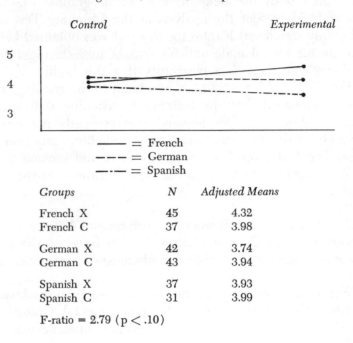

Groups	N	Adjusted Means
French X	45	4.32
French C	37	3.98
German X	42	3.74
German C	43	3.94
Spanish X	37	3.93
Spanish C	31	3.99

F-ratio = 2.79 (p < .10)

Figure 2c.—Progress Test—Listening: Differences in Means
Between Male and Female Subjects

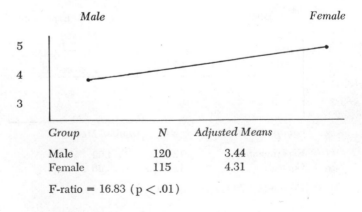

Group	N	Adjusted Means
Male	120	3.44
Female	115	4.31

F-ratio = 16.83 (p < .01)

Figure 2d.—Progress Test—Listening: Differences in Means
Between Male and Female Within Languages

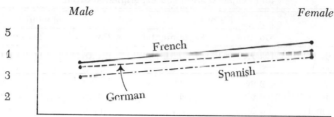

Language	Male		Female	
	N	Adjusted Means	N	Adjusted Means
French	27	3.68	55	4.41
German	57	3.61	28	4.31
Spanish	36	3.00	32	4.14

F ratio = 1.09 (not significant)

Figure 2c.—As has been mentioned above, it seems doubtful that the superiority of the females over the males on this test can be interpreted as a result of either training or exposure to foreign language. Since the relation of achievement on the Listening Test to initial scores on the LAB is extremely slight, as indicated by the regression slope for the pooled equation ($b_p = .03$), adjustment of the Listening Test scores on the basis of initial aptitude could not in any way equalize any superiority of females over males in achievement which may exist regardless of either aptitude training or foreign-language learning. (In this graph, as in Figure 2d, the reader should keep in mind that the difference between the points on the left and right sides of the graphs and the resulting slopes of the connecting lines now represent the differential scores achieved by male (left side) and female (right side) subjects while the differences due to other factors are to be read along the vertical dimension.)

Figure 2d.—The superiority of females over males can be found in all languages. While achievement according to language is ranked (1) French, (2) German, (3) Spanish, the variance due to language does not reach significance.

Table 18 shows the adjusted means for all classes according to treatment groups and sex.

TABLE 18

Progress Test—Listening: Adjusted Means for Male
and Female Control and Experimental Groups

	Female		Male	
	Control	Experimental	Control	Experimental
French 1	3.78	4.28	3.86	3.64
French 2	5.12	4.51	3.03	4.52
German 1	3.86	4.10	3.93	3.05
German 2	4.62	4.71	3.60	3.89
Spanish 1	4.00	4.28	3.30	3.67
Spanish 2	3.30	4.54	1.89	3.12
All Classes	4.19	4.40	3.31	3.58

The detailed results of the analysis of variance for the Grammar component of the progress test are presented with the help of Figures 3a and 3b and Table 19.

Figure 3a.—On the Grammar component of the progress test, the Experimental Groups show a slight superiority over the Control Groups, but this difference is not statistically significant.

Figure 3b.—Within each language, students in the Experimental Groups perform better than those in the Control Groups. Significance is reached, however, by the variation due to language. The graph indicates quite clearly that this is due to the obviously lower performance of the Spanish students. In other words, the pattern of lower performances by the Spanish students noticed on the LAB post-test scores (see Figure 1b above) is repeated, and the same conjectures made in conjunction with the discussion of Figure 1b apply again in this case.

Table 19 shows the adjusted means for all classes according to treatment groups and sex.

TABLE 19

Progress Test—Grammar: Adjusted Means for Male
and Female Control and Experimental Groups

	Female		Male	
	Control	Experimental	Control	Experimental
French 1	9.35	9.20	8.60	9.02
French 2	10.93	10.75	9.26	10.87
German 1	11.11	11.90	9.28	9.29
German 2	8.60	10.69	9.09	10.52
Spanish 1	10.07	8.53	9.54	8.62
Spanish 2	8.12	8.89	6.95	8.90
All Classes	9.76	9.87	8.89	9.60

Figure 3a.—Progress Test—Grammar: Difference in Means
Between Experimental and Control Groups.

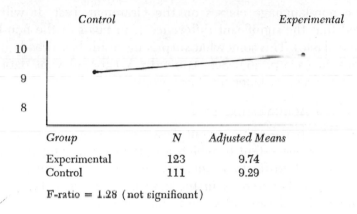

Group	N	Adjusted Means
Experimental	123	9.74
Control	111	9.29

F-ratio = 1.28 (not significant)

Figure 3b.—Progress Test—Grammar: Differences in Means
Between French, German and Spanish Classes.

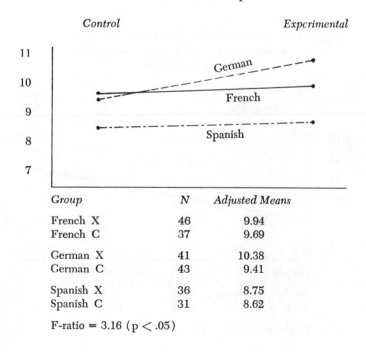

Group	N	Adjusted Means
French X	46	9.94
French C	37	9.69
German X	41	10.38
German C	43	9.41
Spanish X	36	8.75
Spanish C	31	8.62

F-ratio = 3.16 ($p < .05$)

Figure 4.—Figure 4 summarizes the data obtained from the analysis of covariance for the six experimental classes and the three non-language classes on the Grammar Test. It will be noted that the significant difference is in favor of the non-language classes. This somewhat surprising result has already been discussed (see p. 48). See Appendix Vd for relevant data for the analysis of variance for these groups.

Language Achievement Tests

The Language Achievement Tests were designed specifically to measure the extent to which any increase in language aptitude would transfer to an increase in the specific language being studied. Differences in increase of aptitude between Experimental and Control Groups had been slight and had not reached significance. Thus, there was little reason to assume that the language tests would show significant differences between the groups—except for the possibility that continous language training may have a multiplicative effect, increasing initially slight differences in learning ability.

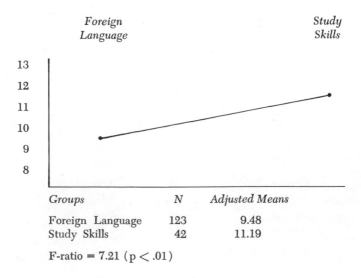

Figure 4.—Progress Test—Grammar: Differences in Means
Between Combined Foreign-Language Classes and
Combined Study-Skills Classes.

Groups	N	Adjusted Means
Foreign Language	123	9.48
Study Skills	42	11.19

F-ratio = 7.21 $(p < .01)$

The regression analyses and the analyses of covariance for the Language Achievement Tests (given in January) and the Final Achievement Tests (given in May) were performed separately for each language since the tests were given in the specific languages the subjects were studying and were thus different in levels of difficulty and in the types of grammatical problems presented. Since only two teachers were involved in each language, the variables of teacher and language were not included in the analyses of covariance, thus leaving a two-way analysis with Treatment and Sex as the sources of variation to be examined. (Appendix Vc summarizes the relevant data for these analyses of covariance.) Scores on the separate components of each of the tests were combined into total scores. The regression analysis for the first achievement test yielded the following figures:

	French	German	Spanish
$b_p =$	.32	.12	.31
$\overline{X}_c =$	51.43	49.58	48.11
$r =$	.35	.14	.30
$F =$	.44	.14	.32

The regression analysis for the final achievement test yielded:

	French	German	Spanish
$b_p =$	.28	.18	.26
$\overline{X}_c =$	51.55	50.07	48.91
$r =$	.48	.35	.39
$F =$	.59	2.14	2.51

Figures 5a and 5b.—These figures summarize the results of the achievement tests administered in the four French classes which took part in the experiment. In both the first achievement test and the final achievement test the Experimental Groups out-performed the Control Groups by a slim margin which fell short of reaching significance. In the first achievement test, both males and females in the Experimental Groups did better than the males and females in the Control Groups, and the difference between Experimental and Control Groups was slightly more pronounced for the male students. In the final achievement test, there was a slight difference in favor of the

Control Group among males and a slight difference in favor of the Experimental Group among females. On both the first and the final achievement tests, girls out-performed boys.

Figure 5a.—Language Achievement Test—French: Differences in
Means Between Combined Experimental and Control Group
and
Differences in Means Between Treatment Groups by Sex

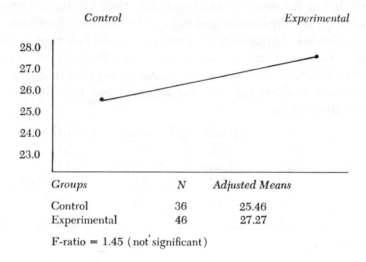

Groups	N	Adjusted Means
Control	36	25.46
Experimental	46	27.27

F-ratio = 1.45 (not significant)

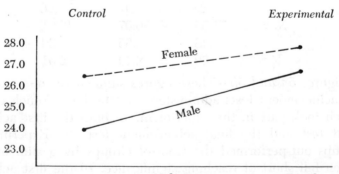

Groups	Male		Female	
	N	Adjusted Means	N	Adjusted Means
Control	15	24.05	21	26.47
Experimental	12	27.02	34	27.37

F-ratio = .41 (not significant)

Figure 5b.—Final Achievement Test—French: Differences in
Means Between Combined Experimental and Control Group
and
Differences in Means Between Treatment Groups by Sex

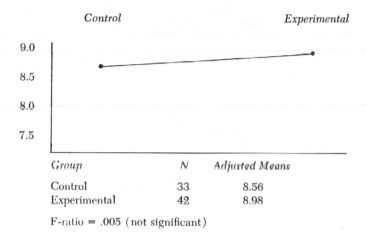

Group	N	Adjusted Means
Control	33	8.56
Experimental	42	8.98

F-ratio = .005 (not significant)

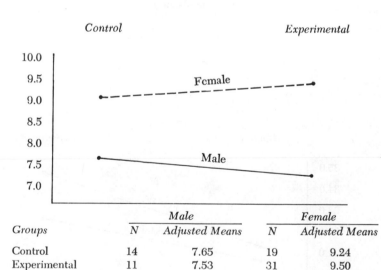

	Male		Female	
Groups	N	Adjusted Means	N	Adjusted Means
Control	14	7.65	19	9.24
Experimental	11	7.53	31	9.50

F-ratio = .022 (not significant)

Figures 6a and 6b.—These figures show the results of the
Language Achievement Tests for the German classes. In both
tests, the pattern in the male and female groups conforms to
the slight superiority of Experimental over Control subjects

Figure 6a.—Language Achievement Test—German: Differences in
        Means Between Experimental and Control Groups
        and
        Differences in Means Between Treatment Groups by Sex

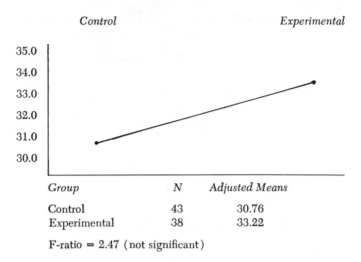

Group	N	Adjusted Means
Control	43	30.76
Experimental	38	33.22

F-ratio = 2.47 (not significant)

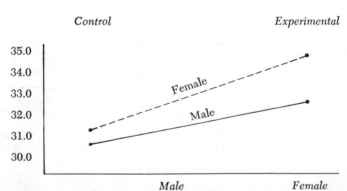

Groups	Male		Female	
	N	Adjusted Means	N	Adjusted Means
Control	28	30.59	15	31.10
Experimental	26	32.57	12	34.63

F-ratio = .19 (not significant)

shown by the total group. Females perform better than males on both tests. Again, the differences between Experimental and Control Groups fall short of significance.

Figures 7a and 7b.— As is indicated by Figure 7a, the first Spanish achievement test is the only language test in which the Control Group has a slight edge over the Experimental Group. The difference in favor of the Control Group is due to the superiority of the females in the Control Group over the females in the Experimental Group. On the final Spanish achievement test (Figure 7b), the Experimental Group is again superior to the Control Group, and the slight superiority of Experimental over Control students is characteristic for both male and female subjects, though the slight difference in favor of the Control Group seems more marked among the males. Again, females score better than males in both the Experimental and Control Groups. Table 20 shows the adjusted means for all classes according to treatment groups and sex.

The results of the language achievement tests can thus be summarized as follows: in five of the six language tests (two French, two German, and two Spanish) administered in the experiment, the Experimental Groups performed better than the Control Groups. The differences in favor of the Experimental Groups seemed most pronounced in the German tests and in the final achievement test in Spanish, but these differences failed to reach significance levels. The pattern of Experimental

TABLE 20

Language Achievement Test and Final Achievement
Test: Male and Female Control and
Experimental Groups

	Female		Male	
	Control	Experimental	Control	Experimental
Language Achievement Test				
French	26.47	27.37	24.05	27.02
German	31.10	34.63	30.59	32.57
Spanish	35.29	32.10	30.58	32.95
Final Achievement Test				
French	9.24	9.50	7.65	7.53
German	14.10	15.70	12.36	14.49
Spanish	14.59	15.11	10.12	14.85

Figure 6b.—Final Achievement Test—German: Differences in
Means Between Combined Experimental and Control Group
and
Differences in Means Between Treatment Groups by Sex

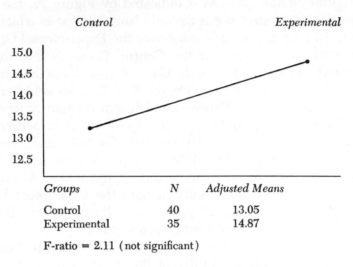

Groups	N	Adjusted Means
Control	40	13.05
Experimental	35	14.87

F-ratio = 2.11 (not significant)

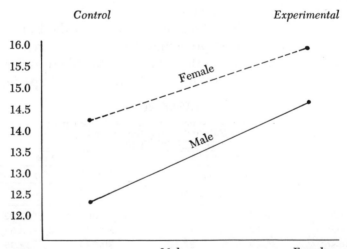

Groups	Male		Female	
	N	Adjusted Means	N	Adjusted Means
Control	24	12.36	16	14.10
Experimental	24	14.49	11	15.70

F-ratio = .04 (not significant)

Figure 7a.—Language Achievement Test—Spanish: Differences in
Means Between Combined Experimental and Control Group
and
Differences in Means Between Treatment Groups by Sex

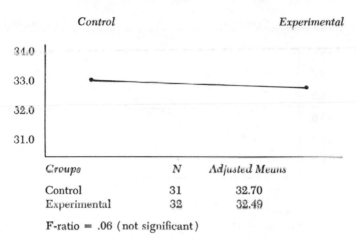

Groups	N	Adjusted Means
Control	31	32.70
Experimental	32	32.49

F-ratio = .06 (not significant)

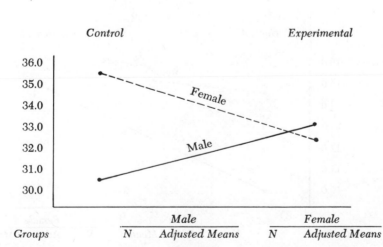

	Male		Female	
Groups	N	Adjusted Means	N	Adjusted Means
Control	17	30.58	14	35.29
Experimental	15	32.95	17	32.10

F-ratio = 2.74 (p < .10)

Figure 7b.—Final Achievement Test—Spanish: Difference in
Means Between Combined Experimental and Control Group
and
Differences in Means Between Treatment Groups by Sex

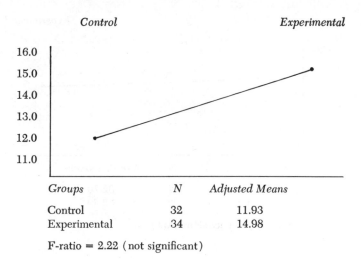

Groups	N	Adjusted Means
Control	32	11.93
Experimental	34	14.98

F-ratio = 2.22 (not significant)

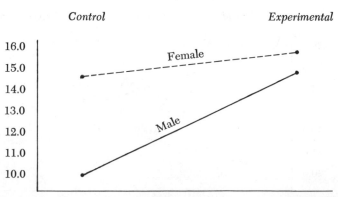

Groups	Male N	Male Adjusted Means	Female N	Female Adjusted Means
Control	19	10.12	13	14.59
Experimental	16	14.85	18	15.11

F-ratio = 1.44 (not significant)

and Control Group achievement in Foreign Language is thus not unlike the pattern revealed by the retakes of the Pimsleur Language Aptitude Battery: a fairly consistent but statistically non-significant superiority of Experimental over Control subjects.

The pattern of superiority of Experimental over Control Groups and its similarity to the pattern found in the results of the Pimsleur Language Aptitude Battery are particularly pronounced among the male subjects. The superiority of the male Experimental Group over the male Control Group in performance on the LAB almost reached significance at the .05 level (see Figure 1e) and male Experimental subjects did better than male Control subjects in five out of the six language-achievement tests, with the difference in one case (Spanish final-achievement test) reaching the .05 level of significance.

An additional check was made on this pattern by means of a t-test of significance of difference between adjusted means (see Elashoff, 1969, p. 12) for the five cases in which the Experimental male means were higher than those of the Control male subjects. Results of this test are shown in Table 21.

It will be noted that significance at the .05 level was reached on the Spanish final-achievement test and that significance at the .10 level was reached on the final-achievement test in German. Since the t-value of 1.29 is needed to reach the .10 level of significance, it may be noted that in all the other cases the differences in fact did approach this level.

TABLE 21

Language Achievement Tests—Male Subjects:
t-Test of Significance of Difference
Between Adjusted Means

Test	Exper. Mean	Control Mean	df	t
Achievement Test (French)	27.02	24.05	77	1.14
Achievement Test (German)	32.57	30.59	76	1.02
Final Achievement (German)	14.49	12.36	70	1.43*
Achievement Test (Spanish)	32.95	30.58	58	1.02
Final Achievement (Spanish)	14.85	10.12	61	1.93**

*p < .10
**p < .05

Since in all of the language tests, the males performed slightly below the level of the females, the probability suggests itself that these differences between Experimental and Control male subjects may be characteristic of the general superiority of Experimental over Control subjects within a lower range of achievement. However, the results of the LAB post-test (Figure le) show quite clearly that the aptitude differences between males and females in the Control Groups are very slight, and that the differences in achievement between male and female subjects cannot be analyzed in terms of differential aptitude.

Summary and Conclusions

Phase II of the experiment confirmed one of the major findings of Phase I—namely, that language learning itself leads to a measurable increase in aptitude. Just as the gains in aptitude of the Defense Language Institute students went far beyond gains that might be due to the retest effect, so did the gains of the students in the Control Groups far outstrip increases in performance that might be due to familiarity with the test.

In addition, Phase II of the experiment demonstrated that not only language learning but also aptitude training will lead to measurable and significant increases in language aptitude. The increases in aptitude scores shown by the "Study-Skills classes" undergoing aptitude training equalled or nearly equalled the gains made by the Foreign-Language classes.

The experiment gave no clear indication that combined aptitude training and language study is superior to language study alone in increasing either aptitude or achievement in foreign language. While, especially in Phase II of the experiment, differences in aptitude as well as language achievement were fairly consistently in favor of the Experimental Groups, only one of the differences was clearly significant, namely, male Experimental over male Control in the Spanish final-achievement test. Various reasons, either singly or in combination with each other, may account for this general pattern of only a slight difference in favor of the Experimental Groups:

a. The training devised in the experiment may not be powerful and intensive enough to influence aptitude significantly above and beyond the influence exerted by initial language training.

b. Aptitude training undertaken in conjunction with a foreign-language course is probably perceived as an extraneous burden unrelated to the objectives of the course and is met with resistance or at least low motivation on the part of the student.

c. Aptitude can be influenced to a certain and limited degree. Thus, the effect of either language training or aptitude training is not appreciably different from the combined effect of both. The already mentioned study by Sturgis which indicates that aptitude and achievement seem unrelated to the amount of exposure to foreign language (Sturgis, 1967) certainly supports the hypothesis that there is a definite ceiling to aptitude increases brought about by the foreign-language learning experience.

Aptitude training that is more powerful and intensive than the training used in this experiment could no doubt be devised. Under what conditions such treatment would be advisable and economical is a different matter. The results of this experiment certainly suggest that for all practical purposes, powerful and intensive language teaching would be preferable to aptitude training in most situations, since it would obviously not only increase achievement in foreign language directly, but would also most likely have the same effects on general aptitude as any aptitude training by itself.

If aptitude training is undertaken, it should not be combined with the foreign-language course. The relatively good showing of the study-skills classes in terms of aptitude gains as well as achievement on the training progress test suggest that aptitude training could serve a useful purpose before students are introduced to a foreign language. Especially for students with relatively low language aptitude, exposure to such training might very well impart certain foreign-language study skills which would prepare them for future language courses.

A very important study which could be undertaken with the help of the training material produced for this experiment would consist of a longitudinal follow-up of two groups of such relatively low language aptitude students: An experimental group receiving aptitude training before embarking upon the study of a foreign language and a control group receiving no such training. The results of this experiment certainly justify the hope that under such conditions—clear separation of initial aptitude training from the language-learning experience—aptitude training would lead to clearly demonstrable superiority in foreign-language achievement.

References Cited

Carroll, John B. "A Factor Analysis of Two Foreign Language Aptitude Batteries," *Journal of General Psychology,* LIX (1958), 3-19.

Carroll, John B. "Research in Teaching Foreign Languages" in N. L. Gage, editor, *Handbook of Research in Teaching,* Rand McNally & Co.; Chicago, 1963.

Carroll, John B. "The Prediction of Success in Intensive Foreign Language Training" in Robert Glaser, editor, *Training in Research and Education,* Science Editions, John Wiley & Sons, Inc.; New York, 1965.

Carroll, John B. and Sapon, Stanley M. *Modern Language Aptitude Test,* The Psychological Corporation, New York, 1958-1959.

Elashoff, J. D. *Analysis of Covariance,* Research Memorandum No. 34 Project 5-0252-0704, Stanford Center for Research and Development in Teaching, Stanford University, August, 1968.

Ferguson, G. A. "On Learning and Human Ability," *Canadian Journal of Psychology,* VIII (1954), 95-112.

Ferguson, G. A. "On Transfer and the Abilities of Man," *Canadian Journal of Psychology,* X (1956), 14-131.

Hatfield, William N. The Effect of Supplemental Training on the Achievement in Ninth Grade French of Students Weak in Sound Discrimination and Sound-Symbol Association Skills, Unpublished Doctoral Dissertation, The Ohio State University, 1965.

Pimsleur, Paul. "Testing Foreign Language Learning (I. Language Aptitude)" in A. Valdman, editor, *Trends in Foreign Language Teaching*, McGraw-Hill Book Company; New York, 1966.

Politzer, Robert L. *Foreign Language Learning*, Prentice-Hall, Inc.; Englewood Cliffs, N. J., 1965.

Sturgis, T. G. *A Study of the Statistical Relationships Between Certain Variables and Success in Learning Certain African Languages*, Unpublished Manuscript; Syracuse, New York, 1967.

United States Department of the Army. *Comparison of the Army Language Aptitude Test with a Commercial Language Aptitude Test*; Adjutant General's Office, Department of the Army; Research Memorandum 59-3, April 1959.

Yeni-Komshian, Grace. *Training Procedures for Developing Auditory Perceptions Skills in the Sound System of a Foreign Language*, Unpublished Doctoral Dissertation; McGill University, Montreal, 1965.

Appendices

APPENDIX II

CORRELATIONS OF PIMSLEUR LAB PRE-TESTS AND POST-TESTS WITH EXPERIMENTAL CRITERION TESTS

	11. Prog Test (Listening) (N=235)	12. Prog Test (Grammar) (N=234)	13. Lang Ach (Completion) (N=243)	14. Lang Ach (Substit'n) (N=241)	15. Lang Ach (Grammar) (N=235)	16. Lang Ach (Reading) (N=239)	17. Final Lang Ach (N=216)
1. LAB Pre-test Vocabulary	.18**	.36***	.04	.03	.20**	.22***	.28***
2. LAB Pre-test Lang. Anal.	.18**	.35***	.01	.05	.01	.16**	.13*
3. LAB Pre-test Sound Disc.	.16**	.22**	.02	.10	.19**	.16**	.22**

4. LAB Pre-test Sound-Symbol	.07	.31***	.19**	.19**	.36***	.21**	.27***
5. LAB Pre-test Total Score	.22***	.45***	.10	.14*	.29***	.28***	.34***
6. LAB Post-test Vocabulary	.26***	.38***	.10	.11	.27***	.30***	.28***
7. LAB Post-test Lang. Anal.	.27***	.44***	.20**	.16**	.19**	.23***	.22**
8. LAB Post-test Sound Disc.	.15*	.26***	-.04	.13*	.10	.21**	.21*
9. LAB Post-test Sound-Symbol	.00	.19**	.02	.17**	.20**	.10	.04
10. LAB Post-test Total Score	.24***	.49***	.12*	.24***	.35***	.35***	.32***

*p < .05

**p < .01

***p < .0005

APPENDIX III
Student Attitude Scale

Language Aptitude Training

The experiment you just participated in was part of a study being conducted at Stanford University. We are very interested in your reaction to it. Could you please give us your honest opinion by putting a checkmark in one of the three spaces after each statement. You do not have to put your name on this paper.

We want you to know that we appreciate your cooperation very much and thank you for being so helpful.

	Agree	No Opinion	Disagree
I learned a lot from the experiment.	____	____	____
The experiment helped me in my language class.	____	____	____
I thought the experiment was interesting.	____	____	____
I thought the material was too easy.	____	____	____
The experiment was worthwhile for me.	____	____	____

APPENDIX IV
APTITUDE TRAINING PROGRESS TEST: UNADJUSTED MEANS AND STANDARD DEVIATIONS FOR ALL CLASSES

	Listening			Grammar		
	Mean	sd	N	Mean	sd	N
Teacher #1 (French) Experimental	4.13	1.4	23	9.08	3.5	23
Control	3.88	1.4	16	9.69	3.6	16
Teacher #2 (French) Experimental	4.54	1.3	22	10.91	3.3	23
Control	4.19	1.6	21	10.57	3.5	21
Teacher #3 (German) Experimental	3.41	1.7	22	10.38	3.5	21
Control	3.91	1.3	22	9.82	3.0	22
Teacher #4 (German) Experimental	4.15	1.6	20	10.70	3.4	19
Control	3.95	1.8	21	8.62	3.3	21
Teacher #5 (Spanish) Experimental	3.70	1.4	17	8.06	3.4	17
Control	3.56	1.6	16	9.69	2.5	16
Teacher #6 (Spanish) Experimental	4.00	1.4	21	8.80	3.9	20
Control	2.33	1.9	16	6.60	3.5	17
Teacher #7 (Study Skills)				9.08	1.4	13
Teacher #8 (Study Skills)				11.61	3.0	13
Teacher #9 (Study Skills)				10.31	3.0	16

APPENDIX Va
ANALYSIS OF COVARIANCE:
PIMSLEUR LAB—POST-TEST

Source of Variation	df	SS	ms	F ratio
Language	2			12.60**
Teachers within Languages	3			2.62*
Treatment	1			.20
Sex	1			.08
Language X Treatment	2			.16
Language X Sex	2			.30
Teacher X Treatment	3			1.92
Teacher X Sex	3			.99
Treatment X Sex	1			3.34
Language X Teacher X Sex	2			2.06
Teacher X Treatment X Sex	3			2.98*
Covariate (LAB Pre-test)	1			289.03**
Error	229	10,746.81	46.92	

*p < .05
**p < .01

Note: Because the cell sizes are unequal, the analysis of covariance is not orthogonal (not balanced), the sum of squares for each effect does not "add up" to the total sum of squares and the tests of each effect are not independent. This is true throughout Appendix V.

APPENDIX Vb
ANALYSIS OF COVARIANCE:
PROGRESS TEST — LISTENING

Source of Variation	df	SS	ms	F ratio
Language	2			2.79
Teachers within Languages	3			1.52
Treatment	1			1.70
Sex	1			16.83**
Language X Treatment	2			2.02
Language X Sex	2			.26
Teacher X Treatment	3			1.09
Teacher X Sex	3			.78
Treatment X Sex	1			.28
Language X Teacher X Sex	2			.36
Teacher X Treatment X Sex	3			1.64
Covariate (LAB Pre-test)	1			6.69**
Error	210	433.87	2.06	

**p < .01

APPENDIX Vc
ANALYSIS OF COVARIANCE:
PROGRESS TEST—GRAMMAR

Source of Variation	df	SS	ms	F ratio
Language	2			3.16*
Teachers within Languages	3			1.04
Treatment	1			1.28
Sex	1			1.51
Language X Treatment	2			.38
Language X Sex	2			.16
Teacher X Treatment	3			1.26
Teacher X Sex	3			.73
Treatment X Sex	1			.26
Language X Teacher X Sex	2			.39
Teacher X Treatment X Sex	3			.06
Covariate (LAB Pre-test)	1			45.31**
Error	209	2,030.35	9.71	

*$p < .05$
**$p < .01$

APPENDIX Vd
ANALYSIS OF COVARIANCE:
PIMSLEUR LAB—POST-TEST, STUDY SKILLS
AND FOREIGN LANGUAGE CLASSES

Source of Variation	df	SS	ms	F ratio
Language	1			1.51
Sex	1			.68
Language X Sex	1			.67
Covariate (LAB Pre-test)	1			186.96**
Error	160	7,742.00	48.39	

**$p < .01$

APPENDIX Ve
ANALYSIS OF COVARIANCE:
APTITUDE TRAINING PROGRESS TEST, GRAMMAR, STUDY SKILLS AND FOREIGN LANGUAGE CLASSES

Source of Variation	df	SS	ms	F ratio
Language	1			7.21**
Sex	1			1.23
Language X Sex	1			.74
Covariate (LAB Pre-test)	1			27.66**
Error	160	1754.86	10.97	

**p < .01

APPENDIX Vf
ANALYSIS OF COVARIANCE:
LANGUAGE ACHIEVEMENT TESTS

Source of Variation	df	SS	ms	F ratio
French				
Treatment	1			1.45
Sex	1			.74
Treatment X Sex	1			.41
Covariate (LAB Pre-test)	1			15.45**
Error	77	3514.29	45.64	
German				
Treatment	1			2.47
Sex	1			.52
Treatment X Sex	1			.19
Covariate (LAB Pre-test)	1			2.80
Error	76	4023.00	52.93	
Spanish				
Treatment	1			.06
Sex	1			1.31
Treatment X Sex	1			2.74
Covariate (LAB Pre-test)	1			12.46**
Error	58	2546.69	43.91	

**p < .01

APPENDIX Vg
ANALYSIS OF COVARIANCE:
FINAL ACHIEVEMENT TESTS

Source of Variation	df	SS	ms	F ratio
French				
Treatment	1			.005
Sex	1			2.02
Treatment X Sex	1			.02
Covariate (LAB Pre-test)	1			23.08**
Error	70	1789.71	25.56	
German				
Treatment	1			2.11
Sex	1			1.31
Treatment X Sex	1			.04
Covariate (LAB Pre-test)	1			8.20**
Error	70	1920.99	27.44	
Spanish				
Treatment	1			2.22
Sex	1			1.82
Treatment X Sex	1			1.43
Covariate (LAB Pre-test)	1			10.97**
Error	61	3022.79	49.55	

**p < .01